# ADVANCE PRAISE

"For as long as I've known Anne Marie, she's been someone who's never been afraid to take on new challenges. Like the great athletes I get to cover, she has thrived at every turn in the road, pushing the boundaries of what's possible. *Cultivating Audacity* embodies her spirit. This book is for anyone ready to make daring decisions and pursue their goals with the determination of a winner."

—MIKE TIRICO, NBC Sports play-by-play announcer and host

"Anne Marie's *Cultivating Audacity* is a masterclass in how to take bold risks and turn them into groundbreaking success. I've witnessed firsthand the power of daring choices, and Anne Marie's approach to strategic growth echoes the same principles that led to great breakthroughs in entertainment, technology, and in so many aspects of life. This book is for anyone ready to step beyond their comfort zone and transform their vision into reality."

—JIM GIANOPULOS, Former chairman and CEO of 20th Century Fox and Paramount Pictures

"From our first meeting, Anne Marie has been a champion and cheerleader, always pushing me to take that next step. Her belief in the power of audacity is contagious, and it's the foundation of everything she teaches in this book. *Cultivating Audacity* is for anyone looking to embrace life with confidence and boldness, just as Anne Marie has done for decades. If you want someone in your front row who believes in you like she believed in me, this book is your guide."

—DANA JACOBSON, *CBS Saturday Morning* co-host

"For more than 30 years, I've seen Anne Marie embody the very essence of audacity. I vividly remember witnessing one of her boldest moves—leaving ESPN to pursue a new life in California. It was a risk that paid off in ways neither of us could have predicted. My dear friend's story is a moving example of what this book teaches: take the leap, trust the process, and extraordinary things will happen. *Cultivating Audacity* is Anne Marie's blueprint for living a fearless, fulfilled life."

— **ROBIN ROBERTS**, *Good Morning America* co-anchor

"I am so glad that Anne Marie Anderson has written this book. I had the honor of working with Anne Marie at ESPN, and she is the consummate professional, and taught me how to be one, too. She has always modeled grit, perseverance, dignity, and grace while always getting the job done at the highest levels of excellence. Anne Marie has literally done it all. She was an accomplished athlete, producer behind the camera, and broadcaster in front of it. Anne Marie Anderson speaks from great experience when illuminating what it takes to accomplish your goals while constantly adapting to and overcoming obstacles, and I always listen. She is the real deal."

— **JAY BILAS**, ESPN college basketball analyst and *NYT* bestselling author of *Toughness*

"In *Cultivating Audacity*, Anne Marie Anderson has written a guide to daring with intention. If you have ever felt paralyzed by hesitation, this book is for you."

— **HEATHER MONAHAN**, Two-time bestselling author of *Confidence Creator* and *Overcome Your Villains*

"Most self-help books are filled with 'you can do it' pep talks that are long on motivation but short of wisdom. *Cultivating Audacity* has both. Let Anne Marie Anderson sit at your side, encouraging you that you were made for more, and showing you step-by-step how she (and you!) can live your most audacious life now."

—LAURA GASSNER OTTING, *Wall Street Journal* bestselling author of *Wonderhell* and *Limitless*

"In *Cultivating Audacity*, Anne Marie empowers readers to assess, adapt, and ultimately take calculated steps toward their biggest goals. This book is an essential guide for anyone ready to ditch the doubt and chase the dream."

—JOHN SPERAW, President and CEO of USA Volleyball and seven-time national champion

"For those who are done with waiting and ready to take that leap, *Cultivating Audacity* provides a road map for action. Anne Marie provides the push and the plan to help the reader find the courage to evolve and thrive."

—HOLLY MCPEAK, Three-time Olympian and NCAA champion

"In *Cultivating Audacity*, Anne Marie offers more than just inspiration; she provides actionable steps for evaluating whether your goals are still in sync with your evolving purpose. This is mandatory reading for anyone seeking clarity and direction in their journey."

—FABY TORRES, Global chief marketing officer at Gap Inc.

"Anne Marie's framework provides readers with the tools to recognize when it's time to make a bold leap. *Cultivating Audacity* is a profound invitation to live boldly and without regret."

—DAN JEFFORDS, USCG command master chief, retired

"*Cultivating Audacity* is about finding your voice, owning it, and never letting anything stand in the way of your potential. Anne Marie shows you how to tap into your inner strength and use it to build a life that reflects your boldest dreams. It's a rallying cry for anyone who wants to break the mold and live unapologetically."

—KATE T. PARKER, Author of *Strong Is the New Pretty*, *Force of Nature*, and *Play Like a Girl*

# CULTIVATING AUDACITY

# CULTIVATING AUDACITY

## DISMANTLE DOUBT
## AND LET YOURSELF WIN

ANNE MARIE ANDERSON

IDEAPRESS
PUBLISHING

WASHINGTON, DC

IDEAPRESS
PUBLISHING

Ideapress Publishing | www.ideapresspublishing.com

All trademarks are the property of their respective companies.

Cover Design: James Jones
Interior Design: Jessica Angerstein
Author Photo: Theo and Juliet Photography

Cataloging-in-Publication Data is on file with the Library of Congress.

Hardcover ISBN: 978-1-64687-169-8

---

**Special Sales**
Ideapress books are available at a special discount for bulk purchases for sales promotions and premiums, or for use in corporate training programs. Special editions, including personalized covers, a custom foreword, corporate imprints, and bonus content, are also available.

1  2  3  4  5  6  7  8  9  10

For Lukas, Grant, and Leyna:

Please clean your rooms.

# CONTENTS

# INTRODUCTION

I think of him often. Yet I didn't even know him well.

In the early morning hours, when my eight-year-old daughter stomps down the stairs, her feet far heavier than her 78-pound body would suggest, I think of him. It's what I remember from his funeral—Peter's father choking through sobs, recalling how his son's feet were always so heavy on the stairs.

Is it weird to still think of him 30 years later? It was a defining moment in my life.

Peter Rogot was a sports anchor at KCNC-TV in Denver in the mid-1980s when I was a teenager interning at the local station, hoping to start a career in television. My memory is foggy regarding the details of that summer, but I shadowed two sports anchors: the nice one and the grumpy one. Peter was the nice one.

After graduating from college, I got a job at ESPN in Connecticut. I was elated and worked my way from a temporary production assistant position to the assignment desk. Peter was hired by ESPN in 1991, two years after me. He would debut in his dream job anchoring *SportsCenter* the following week. He and his wife, Mary, had just moved to Connecticut. They had recently married. The "nice one" with a new wife and his dream job—good things did indeed happen to good people.

As a *SportsCenter* assignment editor, my phone rang constantly. Reporters in need of a satellite truck or a camera crew to cover a story. Random calls from celebrities like Bill Cosby and Dennis DeYoung from Styx asking to come by for a tour or to talk to a particular on-air personality. I became adept at handling the harassing fans calling to complain about the "unfair treatment" their team received on the show. The assignment desk was the main artery of the *SportsCenter* newsroom, and as exhausting as it was, I loved being a part of the action.

On April 9, 1991, a reporter from our former station in Denver called and asked for Peter. I wondered if everyone in *SportsCenter* had met the new guy yet. It was his sixth day on the job. Peter waved at me as he bounced past, headed toward the partition to his new cubicle. Peter was an athlete, an avid cyclist, and in great shape at 37 years old. I transferred the call to his desk.

It was only a few minutes later. Five? Maybe eight minutes? Someone came running around the corner, frantically yelling, "Does anyone know CPR?" There was always so much activity and noise in the *SportsCenter* newsroom that it took a minute to register.

"CPR? Yes, I know CPR."

I sprinted around the corner, expecting to find someone, anyone else, in need of help. But not Peter. Yet there he was, lying on the floor in a heap. Several people rushed to help as we all surveyed the scene. The phone was off the hook, and Peter's sandwich was on the desk with a bite missing. My coworker and roommate, Peggy, was there too. Other people were also helping, but I only remember Peggy, Peter, and me.

We called 911. I remember Peggy checking to see if Peter was perhaps choking. Yes, that would have made sense. Choking can happen even if you are 37 and newly married and fit and starting your dream job. Anyone can choke. But there wasn't any food in his airway. The 911 operator asked questions and assured us an ambulance was on its way. She told us to dump out his briefcase to look for medications. Rummaging through his bag, my hands shook so violently that I had to place each item on the desk to focus on what the item actually was.

At this point, my memory becomes super sharp. Peter was on his back on the ground, I was kneeling on his right, and Peggy was on his left. I remember watching as Peggy grabbed a napkin and wiped her lipstick off. We were starting CPR, and she didn't want to leave lipstick all over Peter's face. Peggy was composed and seemed to always know what to do in any situation. We began. Then Peter exhaled—or it seemed like an exhale at first—but it was the most complete and final expiration of every bit of air and gas and *life* in that human body. I immediately knew this with every cell of my body. It wasn't an exhale. I later learned it is called a "death rattle." It leaves absolutely no doubt that an inhale will never follow. Another breath will never happen. Not for that body. Never.

I stared at Peter, but he didn't look real anymore. It was as if he was made of rubber, unrecognizable. I remember this vividly, and it's the reason I still think often of him.

The ambulance arrived and took his body to the hospital. I say "took his body" and not "took Peter" because I'm certain his soul was already on its way . . . somewhere. Perhaps the EMTs detected a heartbeat? I have no idea. I went to the hospital, though I'm not sure why. I don't recall if anyone was with me.

What I do remember is Mary, his wife. She arrived at the hospital in exercise clothes. "Where's Peter? I want to talk to Peter!" Her voice was laced with panic. She was petite, with dark hair, and her shirt was damp with sweat at the small of her lower back. She had been jogging when someone got ahold of her and told her to go to the hospital. I stared at that sweat stain and thought, *She went for a run and came back to find her husband dead. How cruel is that?* Mary was taken into a room, and I heard her scream. I am in tears now, remembering that scream 30 years later. It was deep, as if it erupted out of her diaphragm, out of her soul. That makes it sound romantic, but it was anything but romantic. It was agonizing, intolerable pain.

My brother came with me to the funeral. The service was in New York, where Peter grew up. It was packed to the rafters with family and friends who were all stunned by the sudden loss. It was an unusually warm spring day, and we parked ourselves in the back of the temple. We didn't want to take a seat away from anyone who knew him better. I strained to see the speakers full of sorrow and hear their stories. I will never forget Peter's father sobbing, recollecting the sound of his heavy feet on the stairs.

I decided then, during that funeral, if you could be 37 and newly married and land your dream job only to have it all ripped away in an instant, I was not going to wait. For anything. Ever. Later that year, I got on a plane and began traveling everywhere my heart wanted to take me. I learned to scuba dive in the Great Barrier Reef in Australia, camped in the Serengeti in eastern Africa, danced in the streets of Belfast, rafted rivers in South America, tracked gorillas in the Congo, and placed offerings to Buddhist monks on the border of Burma all because I didn't want to wait, just in case it all got taken away.

# I WAS NOT GOING TO WAIT. FOR ANYTHING. EVER.

I started to live audaciously. Once I experienced the unpredictability of life, I began to seize opportunities. I made bold decisions. Thirty years later, the knowledge that nothing is promised beyond today still hovers in my daily consciousness.

Too often, our dreams and aspirations are held hostage by the twin jailers of procrastination and self-doubt. We wait for the perfect moment, the right conditions, the stars to align, or the fear to dissipate. We convince ourselves that someday, in the future, we'll be ready. But history is unapologetic in its judgment: Waiting doesn't work.

The longer we linger in the realm of hesitation, the more formidable the barricades against our aspirations become. Excuses pile up, self-criticism deepens, and regret becomes a shadow that dims the radiance of our potential.

*Cultivating Audacity* is a guide to enhanced decision-making. It teaches you to evaluate opportunities and challenges through the lens of audacity, enabling you to make choices that align with your long-term vision and values.

Time spent digging into what stands between you and the life you want is an investment in your well-being. By conquering your fears and pursuing your dreams, you will experience a profound sense of fulfillment and purpose. You will find that audacity leads not only to personal success but also to a richer, more meaningful and joyful life.

It is time to understand the obstacles that stand in our way—the excuses, fears, doubts, and societal expectations that shackle us. In the journey throughout this book, we will confront the limitations that have, until now, dictated our course and held us back from seizing our dreams.

In the moment that Peter lay on the ground before me, his life story complete at age 37, I vowed I would never again wait for the "right time." I still have the same fears all of us have. How am I going to find time for this? What if I fail? I need money and don't even know how to get started, and even if I did, I can't catch up on the work I already have.

In these pages, you will discover practical strategies, empowering stories, and transformative insights that will equip you to confront your fears, dismantle your excuses, and embark on a life-altering quest for audacity.

*Cultivating Audacity* is your invitation to step into the arena of possibility, to break free from the chains of hesitation, and to declare, "Now is my time!"

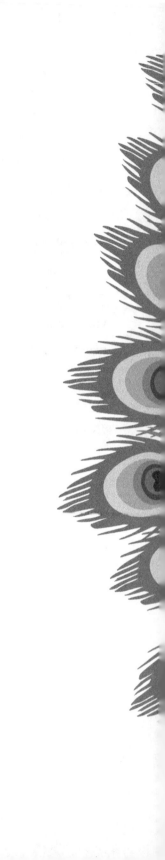

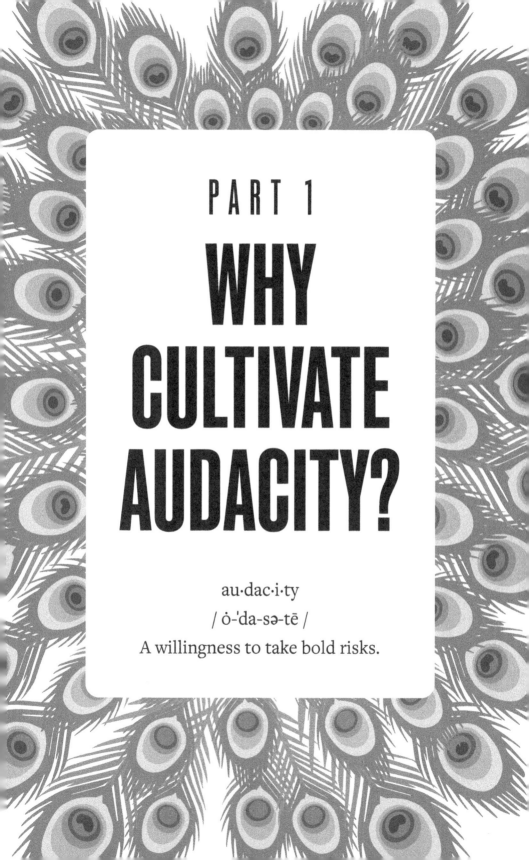

# PART 1

# WHY CULTIVATE AUDACITY?

au·dac·i·ty

/ ȯ-ˈda-sə-tē /

A willingness to take bold risks.

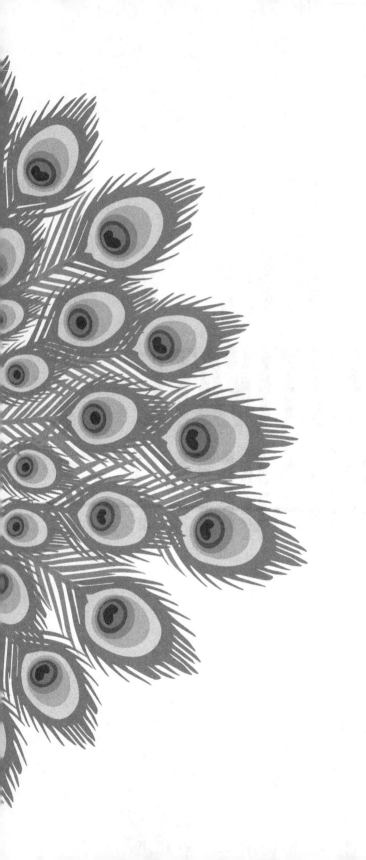

# CHAPTER 1

# THE POWER OF AUDACITY

When I graduated from college, I wanted to work in journalism but was not sure how to make that happen. I knew what I *didn't* want to do—move home and live with my parents. If I didn't find a job, that would be my future. An alum from my university who worked at ESPN visited my class and told us about his career. It sounded fun and exciting, so I asked if ESPN was hiring. He told me the network occasionally hired recent college graduates for a six-month temporary job with no benefits, working six days a week from 6 p.m. to 3 a.m. with Mondays off. It sounded perfect to me! He put me in touch with the HR department and set up an interview.

I borrowed a car and drove from New York to ESPN's headquarters in Bristol, Connecticut, where I was interviewed by a kind man named Al Jaffe. A few minutes after we began talking, he asked what I thought of the Seattle Mariners' bullpen. (A bullpen is a baseball team's pitching staff.) I froze. I didn't know anything about the Mariners. He asked if I could name anyone on the team. I panicked. I couldn't. I stammered and stuttered and never really recovered. At the end of the interview, he politely told me, "I'm sorry, I don't think you are what we are looking for."

I was angry walking back to the car—but not at him. I was angry with myself because I choked! I knew I blew it. After returning to my apartment in New York, I wrote a thank you note. (Because in those days, we actually wrote with a pen on paper.) I licked a stamp, as unsanitary as that now seems, and sent it off. It read:

> Dear Mr. Jaffe,
>
> Thank you for taking the time to meet with me. Unfortunately, I don't think I did a very good job communicating what I could add to ESPN if I were to be hired as one of your temporary production assistants. While I imagine you have a number of candidates who can spit out stats and numbers and years of sports history, I believe I could add a different skill set in that I have already worked in television.*
>
> I respectfully ask you to reconsider, as I would work hard if invited to join your team.
>
> P.S. If I needed to do a story on the Seattle Mariners, I would look it up.

(*Hofstra University, where I went to school, rented out studios at night to a local sports show. They brought in a professional anchor but used students as stage managers, camera operators, and to cut highlights—the same skills I would need at ESPN.)

I didn't have a job at 21, but I had a lot of nerve!

Mr. Jaffe called and offered me the job. After six months, I was offered a full-time position.

Writing that letter was audacious. It was absolutely a risk. However, my other option—moving back home with my parents—was more painful than the probability of being rejected by ESPN a second time.

## Why Audacity Works

Have you ever witnessed someone less qualified than you apply for a job and get it? It is infuriating. We often get angry or annoyed, thinking, *Seriously, he hasn't been here as long as I have*, or *She doesn't have half the credentials I do and* still *got that job?* In reality, we aren't mad at that person as much as we are frustrated with ourselves for not applying. People like to claim that those who don't apply until they have all the required credentials have a confidence problem. I disagree. It's not a confidence problem. It is an *audacity* problem, and it applies to more than job applications. Just as some aren't comfortable applying until they possess 85 to 100 percent of the listed criteria, many people prefer waiting to make big leaps in their lives until the perceived criteria have been met.

What's audacity? The willingness to take bold risks. We hear about glass ceilings all the time, but our desire for change is often stunted by an unwillingness to act until it's too late. You know what they call that? A sticky floor! Picture that image. Stuck to the floor second-guessing ourselves while waiting for the "right time" when we have met all the qualifications, while others leap toward opportunities and get the job despite a lack of credentials. *We need to take more bold risks.*

Often, people are afraid to shoot for the moon for fear of falling short. We all knew that one guy at the bar who kept asking girls out

IT'S NOT A CONFIDENCE PROBLEM. IT IS AN AUDACITY PROBLEM.

until one finally said yes. He didn't quit asking when he was turned down. He just moved on and looked for the next opportunity. If we approached breaking boundaries with the same gusto as that guy, we would all be living audacious lives!

Let's say you and I apply for the same job and have the same qualifications. You are waiting to feel fully qualified before applying, whereas I apply despite having only 50 percent of the qualifications. Generally, I wouldn't get that job with only half of the requested criteria, but in the process of applying, I am also networking and practicing interviewing. Both of us work on adding skills, but I go back a year later and apply again when I have 65 percent of the qualifications. I still may not get that job, but I have had two inside looks at the interview process. Then, if we both apply when we have 85 percent of the credentials, who is most likely to get it? Me. Why? Because I already have a relationship with the people hiring. I have been in front of them three times. I already know the questions that could be asked, and the interviewers have witnessed the growth of my skills.

Applying with 50 and 65 percent of the criteria isn't reckless. It is brave.

## Worth It Versus Reckless

In no way am I suggesting you swing for the fences at all times in all areas of life just to see what lands. There is a difference between reckless risks that can hurt you, your family, your business, and your reputation and "worth it" risks. Quitting your job and moving your family cross-country with no financial cushion or job prospects is reckless. Planning to move your family cross-country after building one year's worth of expenses in your savings account and securing a job might be worth it. A bold move is worth it when its purpose is to get you closer to who you want to be and how you want your life to function.

Audacity involves assessing risks and choosing the ones that are potentially worth it. *Cultivating* means preparation, development, and growth. To cultivate audacity, one must prepare for and develop a habit of taking those worthwhile bold risks. That requires exploring what has stopped you thus far and doing the right kind of preparation before taking that leap. This book will guide you through that process.

## The Components of Audacity

Being audacious involves optimism, courage, and consistency, which correlate to the three components of cultivating audacity: mindset, behavior, and identity.

An audacious *mindset* is a set of beliefs that shape how you make sense of the world and yourself. It influences how you think, feel, and behave in any given situation. It means that what you believe about yourself impacts your success or failure.

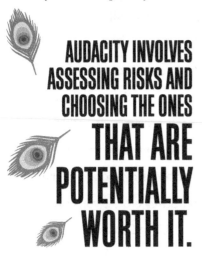

**AUDACITY INVOLVES ASSESSING RISKS AND CHOOSING THE ONES THAT ARE POTENTIALLY WORTH IT.**

An audacious mindset requires optimism. Why does a team down by 12 points continue to compete? Because they are optimistic about the possibility of coming back and winning the game. Will they? Maybe. Maybe not. Optimism is closely linked to confidence. An optimistic person isn't necessarily going to get what they want, but they have the confidence to go for it regardless of the outcome. Win or lose, an optimistic person believes that everything is going to be ok.

Audacity as a *behavior* involves looking for opportunities to take risks and not becoming paralyzed by the potential of failure or rejec-

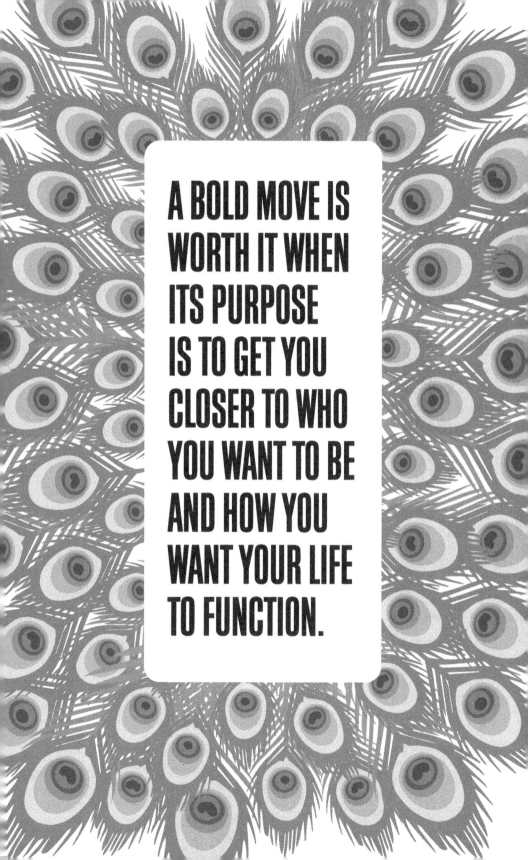

A BOLD MOVE IS WORTH IT WHEN ITS PURPOSE IS TO GET YOU CLOSER TO WHO YOU WANT TO BE AND HOW YOU WANT YOUR LIFE TO FUNCTION.

tion. Audacious behavior requires courageous action. You can sit on your couch all day, being optimistic and thinking about what you want in life, but until you find the courage to act, not a damn thing will happen. Cultivating audacious behavior is an action step. You may read this and say, "I'm willing, but . . ." and that is where we will work to discover and dismantle the excuses keeping you from reaching your goals.

**AUDACIOUS MINDSET ➕ AUDACIOUS BEHAVIOR ➖ AUDACIOUS INDENTITY**

Audacity as an *identity* is a person's sense of self, established by the consistency of their behavior. Identity has continuity—you're the same person over time despite many changes in circumstance.

Building an audacious identity requires both optimism and courage. Once you make one audacious move, it is easier to find the courage to do another and another and one more after that. At some point, the discomfort of practicing an audacious mindset and taking the bold risks that define audacious behavior will subside. Living audaciously and taking risks, both big and small, will permeate your personality. It will become who you are—someone who dreams big and takes the steps to live large despite the possibility of a negative outcome.

Audacious living isn't always about making a big, announced, thoroughly planned move. There are micromoments throughout our day when we can be audacious. Don't want to go to the party all your friends are going to? Say no. Being the outlier is a bold move. It is only a tiny two-letter word but still meets the risk threshold because your friends could reject, ridicule, or ostracize you. (At which point you will dump them, right? You won't change your mind and say, "Ok, I will go for a little bit.") When jumping off a diving board, you are optimistic that you will safely reach the water and swim to the side of the pool. That doesn't mean it isn't scary. This is where mindset (optimism) and behavior (the action of taking a bold risk) meet. When you consistently match an audacious mindset to a behavior, you begin to build your audacious identity.

## Speak Up—To Yourself and Others

What does your inner voice whisper when you think about making a big change in your life? *No, it's too risky, you will look silly, you don't have time, you aren't qualified.* Have you said it out loud? The thing you want to do? Most people I talk to have "the thing"—that career switch they've been wanting to make but haven't found the gumption to do, that side hustle they don't know how to start, that relationship in need of a shift. Sometimes, we don't say the thing out loud because it seems foolish or unreasonable. Dare to say it out loud.

Audacity is daring to think differently. To dress differently. To act differently. It is to answer "We need you to organize all the pictures for the school's yearbook" with a simple "No." Or to look your teenager straight in the eye when they haven't talked with you since last Tuesday but demand, "When is dinner?" and simply say, "I don't know. What are you making?" (They hate that, by the way. Yes, I have done it and 10/10 recommend!)

Audacity is that moment when someone makes a racist or homophobic comment, and you stop the conversation with "Nope! We aren't doing that here. Not acceptable."

An audacious move can be huge, like leaving an abusive relationship, or smaller, like saying no when someone asks you to be on a committee that doesn't serve you.

There is no limit on the daily opportunities to be audacious. In each of those situations—the micro and the macro moves—there is a common thread . . . action. You speak up. You refuse. You do it anyway. You overcome the fear of potential repercussions. What else happens in each of those situations? You take control. You say, "I don't like what is happening here and so I am going to change it."

**LIFE DOESN'T HAPPEN *TO* YOU WHEN YOU ARE AUDACIOUS. IT HAPPENS *FOR* YOU.**

Life doesn't happen *to* you when you are audacious. It happens *for* you. You are the driving force behind your own life.

FOMO is the fear of missing out. I don't have FOMO, but what I do fear is staying the same, stuck in a situation that makes me unhappy. Let's call that FOSS: the fear of staying the same.

Audacity rises when you feel stuck. When the pain of staying the same is greater than the fear of change, it is time to cultivate audacity. If your current situation is not rewarding or energizing, you might be unhappy, or perhaps it is a more subtle "Is this all there is?" feeling.

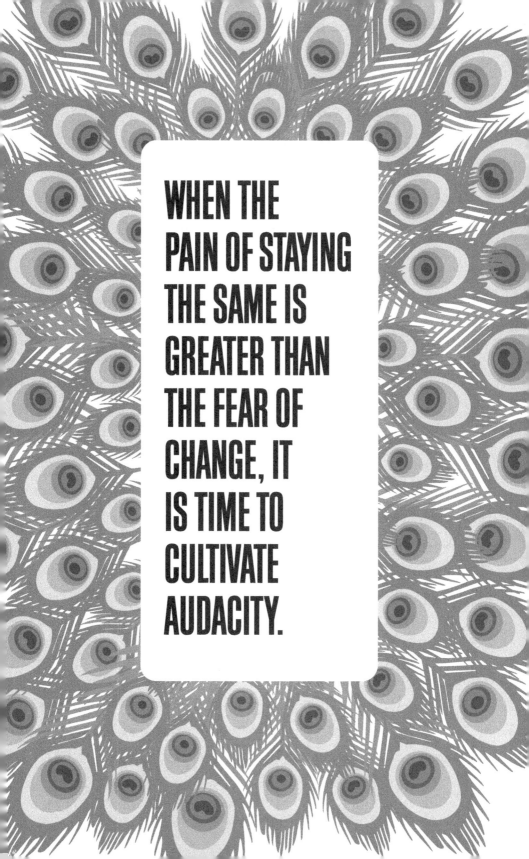

WHEN THE
PAIN OF STAYING
THE SAME IS
GREATER THAN
THE FEAR OF
CHANGE, IT
IS TIME TO
CULTIVATE
AUDACITY.

## The Audacity Continuum

Take a moment to assess who you are today. Consider the status of your current mindset, behavior, and identity. Try to do it without judgment. Where are you in your audacious journey?

What comes to mind when you hear the word *audacity*? It evokes anxiety for some people. For others, it inspires energy. Most people fall somewhere between those two feelings. Think of it as a continuum with anxiety on one end and energy on the other. Where are you?

Reflect on your behavior over the last five years. Have you made any decisions that surprised your friends? Think about your personality as a teenager. Do you consider yourself braver then compared to now? Younger people tend to take more risks than later in life. Were you someone who used to behave audaciously, but time has tamed you?

Consider your identity. Simply put, who are you? How do you fit into your social circles? We all have friends who seem afraid of their shadow and others who throw caution to the wind at every opportunity. How would your peers describe you? Not what you *hope* they would say about you, but who are you in their eyes?

Wherever you are on the audacity continuum, get your feet wet today. Notice the opportunities to practice audacity as you go about your day. Do one audacious thing—right now. It doesn't even have to align with your larger goal. Say no when asked to do something that doesn't serve your purpose. Walk away from a conversation you don't want to participate in. Wear white pants after Labor Day. Do something, anything, unexpected today. It doesn't have to be big. Just *act* in a way different from how you would if you weren't being conscious about audacity. *Be daring.*

Notice how you feel when you make a decision that combines what feels right, lights you up, and is logical. Be aware of your thoughts when you take action, even if it is just a small act. Anxious? Elated? Humored? Proud?

This book is about helping you create a life you are excited to wake up to every day. The average person will have 75 summers, falls, winters, and springs in their lifetime. If you aren't enjoying what you are doing, how you are living, or who you are spending time with, make some changes. Take your fears, hopes, and dreams on a journey to guide you toward who you want to be and what you want to do.

What if you aren't sure what you want to do but know it isn't *this*? Let's figure that out. Turn the page.

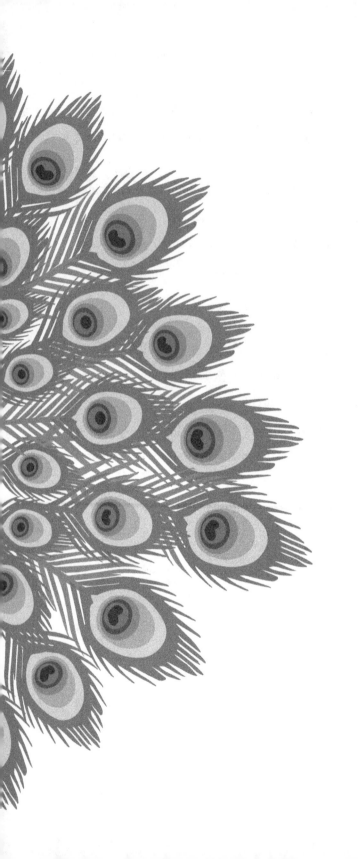

CHAPTER

2

# YOUR TWO LIVES

Five years into my career at ESPN, discontent started growing. It felt like a gnawing undercurrent trying to get my attention. At first, I couldn't put my finger on it. I loved my job and the incredible people with whom I worked. I'd begun my career as a production assistant, putting together highlight packages of assigned games and then writing shot sheets (narrations of the action in a game recap) that Chris Berman, Dan Patrick, or another anchor would read on *SportsCenter*, putting their own style in the delivery.

I remember my brother saying, "So you go to work and watch a game and then pull out all the best parts to create a highlight of the game and then talk about it? That's incredible. I go to my office and work all day. When I come home, I watch a game and then talk to my friends about the best parts of it. I'm doing your job after I finish my job! *Are you seriously getting paid for that?*" Yes, that summed it up perfectly!

Watching games and cutting highlights was just the beginning. After being promoted from a production assistant to an assignment editor, I was deeply embedded in the daily news stories, sitting around a large table in a conference room every morning with men twice my age. The assignment editor always begins the meeting with a list of the top news stories happening, and at 23 years old, I was nervous, researching and writing my notes before presenting them to the executives. I was intimidated but relied on my notes and preparation. "Sudden death round between Mike Donald and Hale Irwin at the US Open. Jimmy Roberts is on-site and has a package on Irwin's premature victory lap yesterday. We are going to get that in at 10 a.m." Or "Andrea Kremer has a sit-down with Evander Holyfield in his home at 3 p.m. We will run it in two weeks on the Friday before his fight with Riddick."

The assignment desk was the pulse of the *SportsCenter* newsroom, and the job was both exciting and exhausting. We editors were tasked with helping ensure producers and reporters were where they needed to be, with camera crews hired according to their specific needs. All

*SportsCenter* content flowed through the desk. The breaking news, well, that was another story. I will never forget walking into work at 2:30 p.m. on November 7, 1991, and hearing that Magic Johnson had called an unexpected press conference. The rumor was he was going to announce he was HIV positive. I had less than 30 minutes to get a camera crew and producer on-site and in the press room. Pure chaos.

I grew to love the chaos. After 18 months, I was promoted to feature producer. My first assignment? Cover the 1992 Summer Olympic Games in Barcelona, Spain. Yeah, baby! I was excited to spend a month in Spain sharing an apartment with Robin Roberts, who was both a friend and an excellent reporter. We had opposite shifts. She worked the normal hours, and I worked until 3 a.m. The days were exciting and challenging. I knew I should love it, and I did, but something was off. I couldn't put my finger on it.

In March of 1994, I took a four-day vacation to visit my brother in California. It was like another world! I had left the cold and snow behind for the beach, where people played volleyball and roller-bladed in the sunshine. I had a great time with my brother watching the waves and walking to dinner, where we ate on a beautiful patio enjoying the ocean breeze. When I flew home, it became clear: I loved my work, but I sure didn't enjoy living in cold weather.

ESPN's headquarters are in Bristol, Connecticut, where winters are tough, and I hated being trapped inside all day. I didn't mind the hours or the demanding work, but I wanted a life outside of work. In Connecticut, I never wanted to leave my apartment because it was always so cold and snowy. Bristol got 83.2 inches of snow in the winter of 1994, which, over 30 years later, still stands as the fourth snowiest winter in 104 years. Yeah. That was not for me. I craved a change.

Shortly after arriving home, I went into my boss's office and announced I wanted to be the Los Angeles bureau producer. "We already have an LA bureau producer," he said.

"I know," I smiled weakly, "that is what makes this conversation so awkward."

We discussed the why behind the sudden request, and then he offered, "Give it two more years here, and if we haven't promoted you to LA bureau producer by then, you can quit and make the move. What will you have lost?"

"Two years," I deadpanned, "in my twenties." I gave him my notice. He called me impatient, and I agreed.

A few weeks later, I drove cross-country from Connecticut to Southern California. I didn't have a job and had no idea what I was going to do. But I knew what I *wasn't* going to do. I wasn't going to shovel snow. I would figure the rest out.

## What's Your Why?

The first step to becoming audacious isn't just identifying what you want to do but *why* you want to do it. What is your motivation? Better lifestyle? More money? Control of your schedule? More time with your family? Recognition from others? Get clear as to what you hope to gain from the change you want to make.

THE FIRST STEP TO BECOMING AUDACIOUS ISN'T JUST IDENTIFYING WHAT YOU WANT TO DO BUT WHY YOU WANT TO DO IT.

Take some time in this chapter to fully vet your motivation. There isn't one right reason to make a change. Everyone has a different rationale, but be careful of external motivations centered on others. Sometimes, we may want to prove someone wrong or make them proud of us. Other times, we seek approval from those we esteem and aim to please them. We may do something audacious or take a risk because we want to put it on social media to impress people. That won't help you here. You can't control if someone is proud of you or even if they will notice the changes you make. Those are external factors that may or may not happen. External motivation isn't what I consider "pure" intention.

**THE INSPIRATION FOR YOUR AUDACIOUS MOVE NEEDS TO COME FROM WITHIN. IT NEEDS TO BENEFIT YOU.**

The inspiration for your audacious move needs to come from within. It needs to benefit you. Even if it provides more money, freedom, challenge, joy, or time with the people you love, all of which may benefit those around you, it needs to improve your current situation. No matter your desired outcome, I urge you to consider the root of your motivation. You may want to achieve something because it will make your mother proud, but will it make you proud of yourself? If you want this change so someone else may think or look at you differently, you will be left unsatisfied. Greatness doesn't spring from extrinsic motivation.

## Envision Your Future

Whenever addressing a group of emerging leaders or soon-to-be graduates, I always begin with that ever-annoying question everyone repeatedly encounters: What do you want to do with your life? I tell them to go ahead and yell it out. Timid at first but increasingly raucous, the audience begins to shout, "own my own business," "criminal defense attorney," "professional chef," "YouTuber," "accountant," and the like. After a minute of that, I interrupt, saying, "Wait, wait, wait! I asked what you want to do with your *life*, and you yelled out a bunch of jobs. Is that all you want from life? A job?"

When dreaming about the change you want to create, consider what your life will look like afterward. What will change? What will stay the same? What will you keep, and what will you let go?

I decided to leave ESPN and move to the beaches of Southern California because I was thinking about my life and not just my job. I had a clear picture of what I wanted my days and nights to look like. I wanted to play volleyball and rollerblade along the beach when I wasn't working. I had to let go of the security of full-time employment and the familiar rhythm of working at ESPN's headquarters to make that happen.

Shortly after arriving in Los Angeles in late July, my former boss at ESPN called to give me some freelance work. ESPN2 had launched nine months earlier, and there was a need for content that fell outside the typical *SportsCenter* stories. My first freelance assignment was to cover a pro surfing tour event in Huntington Beach. I stood barefoot on the beach, interviewing World Surf League Champion Kelly Slater with my toes in the sand. Working without shoes . . . this was an awesome change! I had a pager that would beep and show a phone number on its tiny screen when my supervisor needed to talk with me. I clipped my pager on the net when playing beach volleyball with my friends. When my boss called to give me an assignment, he would always begin the conversation with "What's the score?" He knew what I was doing, and as long as I responded when he paged, he was unconcerned with how I spent my free time.

Being able to play volleyball on weekdays led me to the unexpected outcome of better fitness and health. My days had gone from huddling inside to avoid the weather to a joyful life outside in the sunshine. Within two months, I was busier than I had been when employed full time in Connecticut. O. J. Simpson's trial started, and *SportsCenter* needed a daily presence at the courthouse in downtown Los Angeles. I was often paired with reporter Shelley Smith, covering the day's testimony. By the end of the year, I had doubled my income from what I earned in Connecticut. Money was not my motivation, but the abundance of it was another unexpected outcome.

Within a year of my arrival in California, I was offered a six-month renewable contract by ESPN. I would work for six months and then take a month off to travel. I visited Africa, Ireland, and Australia, each time renewing for another six months upon my return. I was living the life I'd promised myself when Peter died. I was happy, challenged, and exploring the world, and because of the audacious move, I had enough money to enjoy it.

To live the life you want, you need to be able to envision it first. You have to see it before you can claim it. Some people use a vision board to create a vivid picture of their projected future. While you won't have all the answers to exactly what your life will look like, it's vital to envision your projected life.

Believing I've already achieved my goals is the most powerful tool I've used in creating a life I'm excited about. Before going to sleep, I wear headphones and imagine myself in vivid detail, living and working exactly as I desire. The secret is in two tiny words: *I am.* When you move past what your desired outcome looks like to what it *feels* like, your brain activates the same neural pathways as if the experience were actually happening. Your brain believes what you tell it. When you convince your brain the desired outcome has already been achieved, your life flows in that direction.

Sometimes what we don't want is clearer than what we do want. That's ok. Some of us build backward. I remember my college professor announcing to our class of 100 students that, statistically, only one of us would have a career in television journalism despite studying it for four years. When I graduated, I wasn't sure what I wanted to do with the rest of my life if I didn't make it as a journalist. But I knew what I didn't want. I did not want to work in an office or have a job that had anything to do with math. I found technology frustrating, foreign languages confusing, and science beyond my brain's bandwidth. I hated the idea of sales. I couldn't envision myself sitting at a desk all day, but I also didn't want to work outside. I couldn't work in medicine because I fainted at the sight of blood. I knew nothing about business and had no interest in accounting. Other than that, I told myself, I was open to all possibilities!

If that is where you are in the process, then it is time to explore your ikigai.

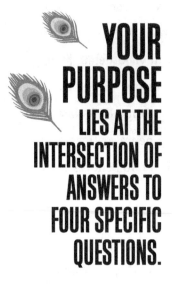

## YOUR PURPOSE LIES AT THE INTERSECTION OF ANSWERS TO FOUR SPECIFIC QUESTIONS.

### Discover Your Ikigai

*Ikigai* is a Japanese concept that loosely translates to your "reason for being." *Iki* in Japanese means "life," and *gai* describes value or worth. The notion is commonly expressed in Western culture through a Venn diagram. The idea is your purpose lies at the intersection of answers to four specific questions.

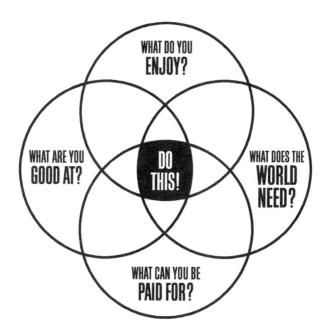

What do you enjoy doing? This can be anything from creating code to spending time with your family to surfing. Literally anything you enjoy doing.

What are you good at? You need to be honest with yourself because if you suck at something, it's probably best not to make an audacious move to force it.

What does the world need? What the world needs is constantly evolving. Did I think we needed people streaming themselves playing video games on YouTube? No, I did not. But apparently, we do because my kids love to decompress from the stress of school by watching other people play video games.

What can you get paid to do? Life costs money. If you are going to dive into an audacious life, you will need to have some dough.

The key to an ikigai is that your answer must meet all four criteria. If you are currently doing three of the four, then it can be a hobby but not your ikigai, and more analysis is required before starting an audacious journey in that direction.

For example, I enjoy gardening. The world needs gardeners. People will pay for someone to tend and cultivate their garden. But I am a horrible gardener. I kill everything I try to grow. (Well, not everything, as the children are still alive. But as far as plants, herbs, and trees go, I am the kiss of black-thumb death.) I have tried everything, including playing music and talking nicely to my plants. They reward me by turning brown, developing root rot, and dying. Last summer, I was buying tulip bulbs in Amsterdam. I was asking a few questions about what tulips need in terms of sun exposure and water when the woman ringing up my purchases pulled the tulip bulbs out of the bag and said, "I'm sorry, these are challenging to grow, and I don't think you are up for the task." True story! The Dutch take their tulips seriously. Gardening is not my ikigai.

I asked my brother what he does well. He said, "I am good at loving my wife." He is so sweet, and indeed, he is good at it. I have no doubt that his wife feels loved and appreciated. And my brother loves being a good husband to his partner. Does the world need people who love their partner? Absolutely. Can my brother get paid to love his wife? Uhhhh, not unless she is a trust fund baby (she's not). So, as much as he is a good husband, and love makes the world better, the man isn't going to feed his family of five and fund his retirement by complimenting his wife's cooking. It doesn't meet the definition of an ikigai. Keep loving, but find something else.

## The Freedom Funnel

It is a lovely concept to think that everyone's career path is at the center of a Venn diagram with answers to those four questions. But I have a problem with that. It only allows for one quest. We are talking about your life, not just a job. There is more than just one answer to your audacious path. The way I earn a living is one area of satisfaction in my life but so is travel, spending time with my children, and maintaining strong relationships.

WE ARE TALKING ABOUT YOUR LIFE, NOT JUST A JOB. THERE IS MORE THAN JUST ONE ANSWER TO YOUR AUDACIOUS PATH.

I like to picture a funnel that contains all your interests and eventually narrows, leading you to a path that brings fulfillment and satisfaction.

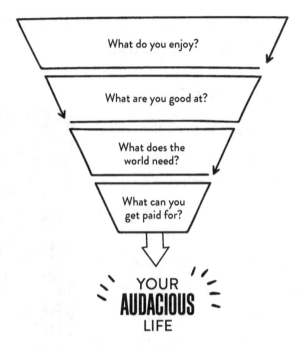

How about you? Grab a piece of paper and write down what you want to create in your life. Then, ask yourself the ikigai questions. What do you enjoy? What are you good at? What does the world need? What can you get paid for?

Start with everything you enjoy doing. Just keep writing until you are out of ideas. From that category, choose the things you are good at. Narrow it down again and write which ones apply to what's needed in the world. Out of what the world needs, what can you get paid to do? When you look at what is at the bottom of the funnel, does it align with the move you want to make? Here is what mine looks like:

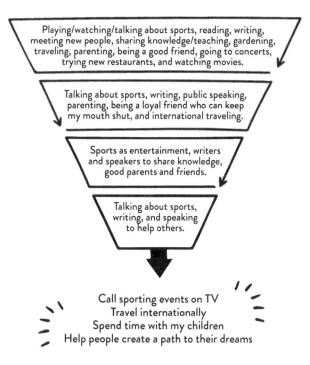

Playing/watching/talking about sports, reading, writing, meeting new people, sharing knowledge/teaching, gardening, traveling, parenting, being a good friend, going to concerts, trying new restaurants, and watching movies.

Talking about sports, writing, public speaking, parenting, being a loyal friend who can keep my mouth shut, and international traveling.

Sports as entertainment, writers and speakers to share knowledge, good parents and friends.

Talking about sports, writing, and speaking to help others.

Call sporting events on TV
Travel internationally
Spend time with my children
Help people create a path to their dreams

What do I enjoy? Anything related to sports, hanging out with my kids, working out and connecting with friends, writing, talking to people I haven't met before, traveling internationally, gardening, cooking, going to concerts, watching movies, and trying new restaurants.

What am I good at? Talking about and playing sports, parenting my kids (most of the time, but we all have days), and talking with people about their lives. I am also a good friend, a good traveler, a good cook, and a decent writer.

What does the world need? Involved parents, loyal friends, great chefs, sports as entertainment, people who want to help others, people who read books, and those who write them.

What can I get paid for? Sports as entertainment, talking with people I haven't met before, and writing.

My current work life: sports broadcaster, keynote speaker, and author.

I don't want my life to be all work, so I added a few things outside my work life, like travel and spending time with friends and family.

Exploring your answers to those questions is a productive exercise to learn how your strengths and values can lead to a fulfilling life. Does the audacious move you want to make give you more of what you enjoy? More time with your children, more money, more joy, more freedom?

**DOES THE AUDACIOUS MOVE YOU WANT TO MAKE GIVE YOU MORE OF WHAT YOU ENJOY?**

This exercise also allows you to examine what you want in this life. If you don't know what you want, and you are stuck in unhealthy relationships, debt, a job you don't enjoy, a zero-balance bank account, or not loving the skin you are in, then what is the point of making money and staying safe? When you allow yourself to truly define your desires and say, I do want money, time, freedom, and creativity, then you're on the right track. Then, and only then, is it time to devise a plan for how to live that life. A plan is what fosters change, and this book will help you formulate that plan and a path that brings joy.

## Compare Your Two Lives

Considering what your life would look like without any change is just as powerful as envisioning your audacious future. If you let comfort or fear dictate your path and stay stuck, what might that look like? How would you feel if you never tried?

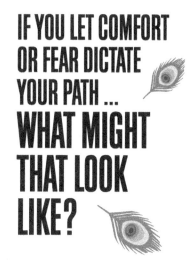

**IF YOU LET COMFORT OR FEAR DICTATE YOUR PATH ... WHAT MIGHT THAT LOOK LIKE?**

The contrast of those two lives will help you on your decision-making path. Being honest with yourself is crucial when considering the "What if I do" versus the "What if I don't" scenarios. Try this exercise in comparing your two lives—the one you have now and the one you could have by making the move of your dreams, whether that be starting a business, leaving a toxic relationship, making lifestyle adjustments, or starting a new job.

Consider your current situation:

- How do you feel when waking up each morning? Are you looking forward to the day? Or just existing or surviving?
- What is your stress level? Your financial situation? Your attitude toward the work you do? Do you have a relationship? If so, how does it help you grow?

- What do you do outside of work?
- How often do you smile throughout the day? (I know that one is a stinger, but it is a good indication of joy, or lack thereof, in your life.)

Define what you want to do:

- Be specific in not only defining the change but also how you think it will improve your life.
- Get clarity on your motivation and whether it is intrinsic or extrinsic.
- Make your goal measurable, whether it is more time with your family, greater financial security, travel, or occupying a specific role in an organization.

Envision your future if you make the move:

- What would your relationships look like? Not just romantic relationships, but with your family and friends as well.
- In a best-case scenario, what would your financial situation be? How would that impact your day-to-day living?
- In your new situation, how would you spend time outside of work?
- How do you feel when picturing that new life? Dive into the feeling of a day in your new life. Would there be more time for joy?

What might happen if you never find the audacity to take the risk to get the life of your dreams? Go there. Go all the way into the question, What might I think at the end of my life knowing I never tried? What would it feel like to approach the end of your life wondering what might have happened if you had taken more risks?

My mother is 93 years old. One day she told me, "Anne Marie, I envy you. I always wanted to work outside the house but never figured out how to do it." I can't decide which part of that statement makes me more emotional: the fact that my mother set her dreams aside to raise my siblings and me, or that I always thought my mother must think I'm not a good mom because I travel and spend nights away from my children. She said, "You are brave. I was always afraid of what other people might think." That was all the validation I needed to know my children are happy because their mother is happy. My children take risks because their mother takes risks. Our children are watching. Give them the gift of being brave.

By now, you have a good idea of what you want and why. What comes next? *But.* But I don't know how. But I don't have time. But I don't have enough money. But what if I fail? We all have those stories holding the door to our dreams tightly shut. Let's crack the door open. Turn the page.

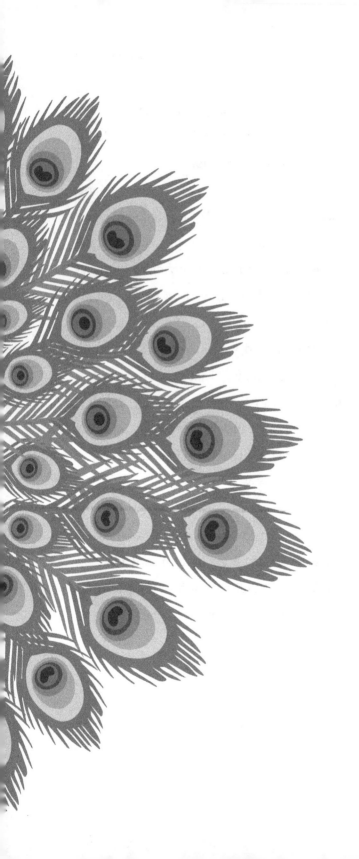

CHAPTER

3

# IDENTIFYING BARRIERS

As the youngest of five children, I followed my four brothers everywhere they went. Whatever sport they played, I played. When they took piano lessons, so did I. When my brothers went to church to become altar boys, I went with them.

There I was, six years old, in a room full of prepubescent boys for our church's annual meeting to recruit altar boys. My oldest brother, Ed, was 12. Dan, Steve, Gary, and I sat neatly in a row next to him.

The five of us were born within six and a half years of each other, and we were a tight crew.

A priest instructed everyone to introduce themselves by saying their name, age, and why they wanted to be an altar boy. One by one, the boys stood up as instructed, some speaking with trembling voices and others with great confidence. When the wave of introductions got to our row, Ed rose. "My name is Ed. I am 12 years old, and I want to be an altar boy because I want to serve the community." Next it was Dan's turn, followed by Steve and Gary.

Since I always followed Gary, naturally, I stood up and, in my loud six-year-old voice, proudly announced, "My name is Anne Marie. I am six years old, and I want to be an altar boy because . . ."

Laughter erupted throughout the room. The priest chuckled and said, "You can't be an altar boy."

"Why not?" I asked. My face was hot and flushed from being the butt of a joke I didn't understand.

"You aren't a boy," he stated kindly.

"Ok, then I want to be an altar *girl!*" Another roar of laughter, this time even louder. Even my brothers were laughing at me. My eyes stung with tears and frustration as the priest explained that girls could not be altar servers. I was embarrassed. That is one of my earliest childhood memories.

At that moment, I developed a fear of being embarrassed in front of large groups of people. I carried that fear with me for decades and let it stop me from taking risks. Only after connecting that story to my reluctance to try new things was I able to move past it.

Being audacious is key to creating the life you want. After comparing your two lives in chapter 2, you should have a good idea about what you want and why you want it. So why haven't you already done it?

# YOUR STORY IS WHY YOU AVOID THE WORK LEADING TO THE LIFE YOU WANT.

## What's Your Story?

Unearthing what stands between you and the life you want can be uncomfortable work—so much so that we avoid it. There is a story you have been telling yourself that has blocked you from doing the work to get where you want to be. It is about who you are and why you act and behave as you do. Your story is your security blanket. It is the reason "why": Why you're doing the things you do, are married to the person you're married to, are living where you live. It is why you avoid the work that leads to the life you want.

That story or stories are your limiting beliefs. They are the barrier between you and the process of creating your other life, the one that made you pick up this book. You are on your way to making the necessary changes to living that dream, but you can't get there until you do the uncomfortable work of diving into what has kept you stuck. There is a reason behind your current circumstances, and if you want to change them, it is imperative to understand how you got to where you are.

Simply put, those stories are a wall you built and now must deconstruct.

## The Four Big Barriers

The four most common barriers to making an audacious move are fear, time, money, and the inner critic. Why are those four obstacles universal? Why do we let them carry so much weight? Because our brains are built to protect us. It is quite literally the function of the amygdala to alert and protect us from harm. We are wired to seek comfort.

Barriers are not inherently bad. Just as guardrails on mountainous roads protect cars from falling off a cliff, our excuses serve as a type of blockade to protect us from making reckless decisions. The difference between a risk that is worth it and one that is reckless is the difference between a happy, satisfying life and one that feels chaotic and out of control.

Fear was my barrier. That memory of being laughed at in the church stuck with me. I was afraid to put myself out there and risk people laughing at me when I tried something new. Such a small moment as a child had a lasting impact. I felt humiliated, with all eyes watching as I stumbled. Maturing into adulthood, I was afraid to fail, be embarrassed, be judged, sound stupid, and be bad at my job. Fear had such a powerful seat at my personal table that I waited 10

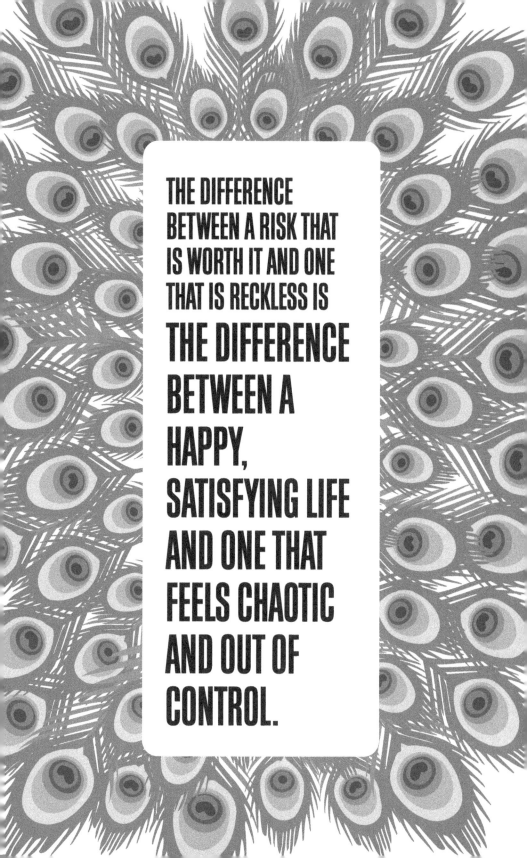

THE DIFFERENCE BETWEEN A RISK THAT IS WORTH IT AND ONE THAT IS RECKLESS IS **THE DIFFERENCE BETWEEN A HAPPY, SATISFYING LIFE AND ONE THAT FEELS CHAOTIC AND OUT OF CONTROL.**

full years at ESPN before I told anyone I wanted to work in front of the camera. I produced for reporters every day and sometimes wrote copy that others repeated on air. I instructed them on how to adjust their delivery for more impact and made sure they looked good on air. Why was I so afraid to do it myself?

I told myself a story about moving from producing to reporting. *People will think I am vain, and it is difficult to get an on-camera job, so I might not even be able to do it. If I do get a job on television, I open myself up for embarrassment and humiliation if I am not good at it. People might criticize me, and that will hurt my feelings. I must protect my feelings at all costs because if I don't . . . what? I will be embarrassed, and I don't ever want to experience that feeling again like I did when I was six years old.*

Overcoming barriers is always about assessing the risk. I'm not suggesting you quit your job, uproot your family, and move cross-country to start a new endeavor. That qualifies as a reckless risk without serious planning and strong support systems in place. Weighing the risk versus the potential outcome is a huge part of living audaciously. The worst that could happen to me if I were bad on air was being embarrassed and not getting hired again. It was a risk worth taking. The story my inner critic was telling me was just that—a story. And a fictional one because it predicted a future that had not yet happened.

### Fear

When fear is the obstacle, I always advise people to do the thing they fear most first. Go fail right out of the gate. Fail the test. Bomb on stage at the comedy club. Get turned down for the job. A fear barrier is always about the outcome. Putting yourself in a situation where failure is likely and then surviving that failure makes the next attempt less frightening. It will never again be your first time. More on that in chapter 4, "Make Friends with Fear."

### *Time*

How often have you said, "I want to, but I don't have time"? No one with a goal, and I mean no one, has spare time. If they say otherwise, they don't have any measurable intention of achieving that goal. Most of us are already overwhelmed with days packed to the brim. How can one more thing be added to an already packed schedule? People with no kids, no pets,

OVERCOMING BARRIERS IS ALWAYS ABOUT ASSESSING THE RISK.

and no plants don't have time. People with two jobs and four kids don't have time. You have to find time—not "make" it but rather carve it out. Easier said than done? I feel the same.

I put off writing this book for two years because I have three children, a full-time television career, and keynote speaking engagements as I travel zigzagging across the country. I get it. Let me just acknowledge that, like most of you, I can handle my work life. It is the abundance of bills, doctor's appointments, sports, art projects, family gatherings, cooking, cleaning, and what seems like 300 school emails per week that tip me over the edge. Finding time to write a book? That was an issue. In chapter 5, we will discuss how to create some boundaries around time and separate what is urgent from what is important. It is a different way of prioritizing, and it works.

## Money

Others identify money as their primary barrier. Not enough of it. Scared to spend it. The belief if you desire money, you are materialistic. There are many reasons why finances are often an obstacle, and they all follow the word *but*: I want to, *but* I don't have enough money. But I feel bad asking for money for that. But what if I don't earn enough money to live when I make the move? If finances are one of your barriers, then a deep dive into your family's history surrounding money is step one. A look at your financial picture and careful budgeting is step two in evaluating worth it versus reckless decisions. "Money is no object" is a lie unless you are independently wealthy. I'm not saying that money is just material or to throw caution to the wind. But I am saying that money should not stop you from starting. When I detached my self-worth from the decision-making process and asked for help, I made some headway. More about that in chapter 6.

## Inner Critic

Our inner critic can be a formidable foe. That voice constantly whispers caution or criticism about what we believe about ourselves. What we are capable of, what we deserve, whether we even belong in the room. It can make us question every decision we make. It whispers, "I can't," when things get hard. That voice is a master at composing a list of reasons you shouldn't make the move. As soon as you dispel one, another pops up like a whack-a-mole trying to talk you out of your scary leap. Missy West, creator of Crush the Inner Critic workshops, teaches audiences nationwide how to identify the negative stories you tell yourself. Quell your inner critic. Pay attention to the things you are telling yourself. Once you track the thoughts that keep popping up for you, West recommends having a conversation with that voice. Sound crazy? Not really. Those thoughts are separate from who you are. "They aren't real. This is literally you making up a story that has no basis in reality," West says.[1] In chapter 7, West dives in with us on specific steps to crush your inner critic.

## Evolving and Reevaluating

Even when you have identified and addressed the obstacles to the life you crave, it is important to reevaluate occasionally. I have taught myself to keep track of my level of engagement and contentment at varying points to ensure new barriers don't arise.

For 11 years of producing at ESPN, I loved my job. I felt like Forrest Gump, always at the center of the biggest story. I thrived working at the biggest sporting events in the world, and it made me feel included in the stories most people were talking about. It was a bonus that my coworkers became my friends. We were in the thick of it together. O. J. Simpson trial? Heavyweight title fight? Superbowl?

Olympics in Norway? Where is my ticket? I'm in! Let's go! Until, over time, I felt unfulfilled.

A similar drop in contentment happened when returning to my work as a play-by-play announcer once games were reinstated after the pandemic. I loved sports broadcasting and swore I could do it every day for the rest of my career, but after Covid, networks slashed pay, and I returned to a game rate lower than a decade earlier. I took on extra games so I could make up the financial difference, but my interest started to wane when I couldn't prepare as thoroughly as I wanted. I decided to take fewer games so I could do a better job and add in the new challenge of keynote speaking.

How did I know I needed to make that change? Because I had been there before. I had loved my job as a sideline reporter and then as a play-by-play announcer so much that I woke up with a huge smile, knowing gameday had finally arrived. I had butterflies and couldn't wait for the game to start. That evaporated when I was no longer paid what my decades in sports broadcasting deserved. The market decides how much you should be paid. You can paint a portrait and think it is worth $300,000, but if the best offer you get is for $500, then that is what it's worth. People were flooding into sports broadcasting, and with traditional television shrinking while streaming grew, networks could afford to hire less experienced broadcasters for a quarter of what I was making. I wasn't angry that the network rates were reduced, but I didn't want to be resentful about going into work. I wanted to work with joy.

I made a calculated risk to pursue more keynote speaking opportunities so I could set my rate and determine my own value. I still do television because I love it and am pretty good at it, but I have given myself the option to accept only the games that bring me joy. Those moves come naturally for me now that I have identified my barriers and morphed my inner critic into my inner coach!

Let's do the same for you.

Try this exercise to dig into why you haven't done "the thing" yet.

Grab a piece of paper and create four columns. Across the top, label each column with one of the four barriers: fear, time, money, and inner critic. Write under each label every story you can think of related to that obstacle.

For example, as I considered making the move to reporting in front of the camera, my column under "fear" looked like this:

- People will think I am vain.
- It is hard to get a job on TV.
- People will judge me.
- I will be bad at it and embarrass myself.
- I don't have enough talent to be on air.
- Strangers will be able to criticize me.
- I will fail and won't have a job at all.
- I have no idea how to start.

Some fears result from an outer critic (family, friends, colleagues, people on social media) and some from your inner critic (I will be bad, I'm not talented, I don't know how to start).

After completing the exercise, step away from it. Get a good night's sleep and look at it in the morning with fresh eyes. Where do you see barriers? What is the story you have been telling yourself? Is it fear, time, money, or your inner critic? It can be more than one, and most likely, it is a combination of a few or all of them. Take that information into the following chapters.

**AUDACITY IS NOT THE ABSENCE OF OBSTACLES BUT THE DETERMINATION TO OVERCOME THEM.**

If the thought of doing the uncomfortable work of digging into your past seems almost too much to face, ask yourself what price you're paying for *not* making the change. Are you waking up dreading the day, living paycheck to paycheck, counting the hours until work is over, or existing in a relationship where you aren't valued? When you shift from waking up to a life that is "fine" to envisioning what your days and nights could look like, your future begins to unfold.

Congratulations! You have done the hard work of identifying your barriers. Part 2 will guide you through the necessary steps to help you move past them. Please don't shy away from the uncomfortable truths. Trying to excavate your story as to why you haven't yet done "the thing" can be difficult, but a life you love is on the other side of it. Audacity is not the absence of obstacles but the determination to overcome them. Keep going. Turn the page.

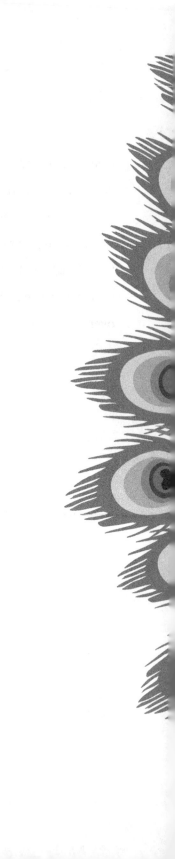

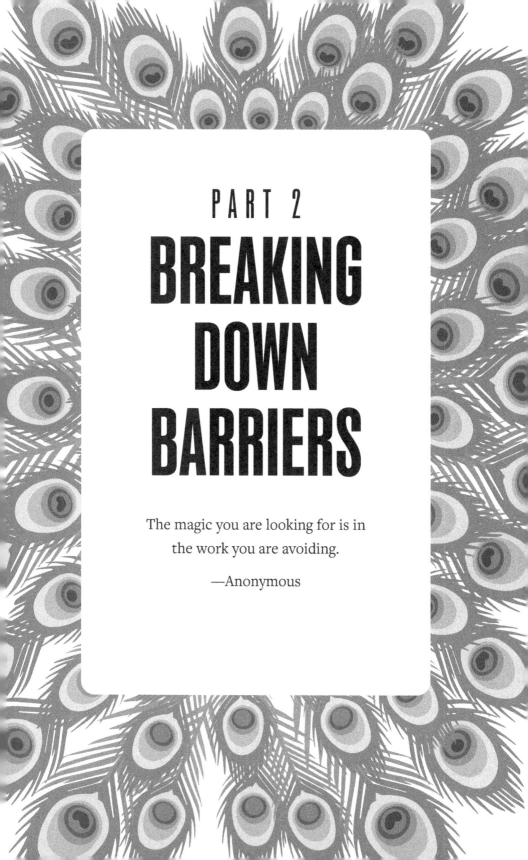

# PART 2
# BREAKING DOWN BARRIERS

The magic you are looking for is in
the work you are avoiding.

—Anonymous

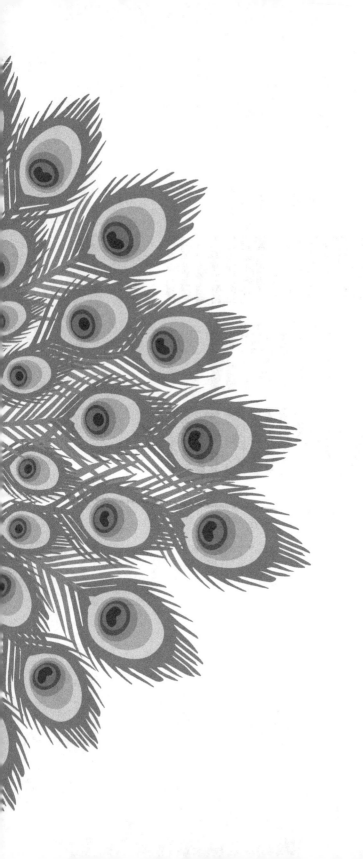

# CHAPTER 4

# MAKE FRIENDS WITH FEAR

My first time on live television was in 70 million homes.

*That* was not the plan. I had been hired as a sideline reporter on ESPN's regional television network, but a colleague called me before I ever went on camera. She was a very successful sideline reporter for ESPN who could not do some of her assigned games. She told me, "I have a conflict with several games. I am going to call Ed and tell him I can't do them. You should call him in five minutes and ask if any other games are available."

So I called. "I'm looking forward to the season. If anything else becomes available, please think of me!"

He answered, "Actually something *did* just become available!" and I was assigned her games.

My first college football game was on ESPN2—not exactly starting small. I was out front in a national game with a massive audience. In the years prior, I had produced coverage of dozens of college football games, but this would be my first time in front of the camera on live television. I'd been working college and NFL games for the better part of 14 years, so maybe my colleagues assumed I had been on live TV before. I hadn't, and I panicked. Recalling it decades later still makes me a little anxious. It was sheer terror that I would embarrass myself in front of millions of people.

Moments before the game, my phone rang. It was the same friend who had tipped me off about backing out of her games. She asked how I was feeling. "Not good, not good at all! I'm pretty sure I'm about to throw up on national television," I whispered to her.

She advised me to take some deep breaths and assured me, "No matter how bad your first time on television is, it won't be as bad as mine." Really? She had been a successful reporter for several years. She was beautiful and polished, and everyone loved her. I couldn't imagine her having a problem.

The role of a sideline reporter is to be the eyes and ears of the viewer on the field. What would the viewer never know unless you were down there to tell them? In my friend's first game, the visiting quarterback was in the national conversation for the Heisman Trophy, college football's most prestigious award. The guys in the booth—a play-by-play announcer and analyst—were talking about the quarterback and mentioned he was a potential Heisman candidate. My friend told the producer, "I can add." (That is how a sideline reporter lets the producer know they can support or expand on something said on the broadcast.)

The producer instructed the play-by-play announcer to bring in the sideline reporter, "For more on this story, let's send it down to the field."

Proud to contribute something that no one would know if not for her, she began, "Guys, I know you are talking about him as a potential contender for the Heisman Trophy, but the fans down here disagree. They are chanting, 'Heisman my ass, you suck, you suck!'" She paused, then, "Bob, back to you!" I burst out laughing!

Uhhhhh, yeah, she was right. I wasn't going to swear on live television! And she still had a job, even after that gaffe. How bad could I be? That story was enough to calm me down, and I walked out to the field. The moment came for my opening report, and I carefully maintained eye contact with the camera and slowly repeated the report I had memorized. I was terrible—stiff and unsmiling—but I didn't curse on camera. Victory! And I did it—I faced my fear of embarrassment and reported on camera. The only thing that was better the second time was that it wasn't the first. I was terrible the second time, the third, and the fourth. But each week, I got out there despite being afraid. I learned that day to make friends with fear.

## Examine and Embrace Your Fear

Fear is an invitation to grow. Of course, that growth can hurt more than passing a kidney stone, but it is still progress. Before becoming aware of the power of embracing fear, I'd do anything possible to

**FEAR IS AN INVITATION TO GROW.**

turn it away, bury it, avoid it. It was such an awful feeling—an unease in my stomach, chest, and head. When I decided to change my relationship with fear, I challenged myself to tune into the discomfort. I began to pick at it, examining my fear with a neutral curiosity. What was it that I was

fearful of? Rejection? Failure? Embarrassment? Judgment? Or something else entirely?

Perhaps most importantly, I stopped shaming myself for feeling fearful. It is natural to avoid fear. It can signal danger. Healthy fear can save lives: backing away from a venomous snake. Deciding to pull over on a snowy mountainous road. Crossing the street when you see a growling dog. Those are all excellent reasons to be fearful. When our internal alarms go off in response to an outside threat, the best course of action is absolutely to proceed with caution. When fear is a barrier to living your audacious life, however, it's crucial to recognize how these fears can paralyze progress. Fear exists to protect us, but it can also be a liar.

## Lies Fear Tells

Fear lies about what could happen even before we take action. Fear as a barrier manifests in various forms, none of which is a certain outcome. Fear of judgment happens entirely in the head. It assumes the feelings and thoughts of someone else,

# FEAR EXISTS TO PROTECT US, BUT IT CAN ALSO BE A LIAR.

which may or may not be true. Fear of the unknown is based on the projected results of an action that has not yet occurred. Recognizing how these fears can paralyze your progress is the first step toward breaking free from their grip.

Making a decision from a place of fear is a weak thread. It's playing defense, reacting to something that hasn't happened. When you make an offensive move, the prospect of failure is just one item on a menu of possible outcomes. What's an offensive move? It is when you take action. The desired result may or may not happen, but you are on offense by deciding which direction to go. When a decision is fear-based, such as staying in your current situation because you are afraid of the unknown, the only possible outcome is to stay the same. We may think staying where we are is safer than taking the risk, but it is actually the opposite. Staying the same isn't safe; it ensures no growth is possible. An offensive decision generates the potential for growth and increases your chances of success a thousandfold, even if it doesn't work immediately. The success is in the decision to act in the face of fear, not in the outcome.

**STAYING THE SAME ISN'T SAFE; IT ENSURES NO GROWTH IS POSSIBLE.**

To prevent fear paralysis, do the thing that scares you most first. With my first time on television, I was afraid I would be terrible (true), it would be embarrassing (true), and I would never get another chance on television (not true). Doing the thing that scares you most first makes everything that follows easier because you have already failed once, and it didn't kill you or ruin your life.

## Fun with Rejection

Yes, I meant what I said: It is possible to have fun with rejection. Television is a tough business. I can't count how many times I have gone after a job, an assignment, or a position and been rejected, but it took a while for me to see rejection as an opportunity. It was an opportunity to fail, survive, and carry on. After I made friends with fear and accepted it as a necessary part of the growth process, I actively sought out situations where rejection was likely. I thought of it as practicing audacity—they couldn't fire me if they hadn't hired me yet.

When I first moved to Los Angeles and got the contract with ESPN, I could work for other networks if it didn't conflict with my current assignments. I wanted to work with the Fox network, but had heard from several people that the man who did the hiring was a bully. This was undoubtedly an opportunity for rejection, so I was prepared when I went in to talk with him. Ray was as advertised: dismissive and utterly disinterested in what I had to say. I left the interview proud of myself for pursuing a conversation even though I assumed rejection was a foregone conclusion. Examining my feelings after the encounter, I wasn't upset but curious. What would happen if I tried again? And again? As for practicing audacity and being rejected consistently, I had found my man. I decided to mess with Ray a little bit.

Every time we were at the same event, I approached Ray, reintroduced myself, and asked if today was the day he would hire me. "Hi there. I'm Anne Marie Anderson. We've met before. Is today the day you are going to hire me?" Just like that.

The first time I did it, he scowled and grunted, "No."

Three months later, passing him in the hallway heading to a press conference, I asked again if he had work for me. He looked away. Every time I saw him, I did the same thing. I would catch his eye across the room and wave with a smile, pointing to myself and mouthing, "*Is today the day?*" Eventually, he laughed and wagged his finger at me because I was so crazy. He also knew I wasn't intimidated by him.

A year later, sure enough, he approached me at an event and said, "Today is the day. I have something for you. Let's talk!"

Ray assigned me to a basketball game as a sideline reporter. Afterward, he was pleased and told me what a wonderful job I had done. His praise was gratuitous, as I only did a handful of 20-second reports on camera. It felt disingenuous, and I wondered why he was so effusive over a minor contribution. Ray offered me another assignment, hosting the Pac-12 Conference Women's Basketball Tournament show. I accepted even though I had no prior experience hosting a remote show. One of the unspoken rules in television is that you say, "Yes, of course I can," to anything you are offered or asked to do, and then you just figure it out. Never turn down a job. That is audacity—saying yes and figuring it out.

**AUDACITY IS SAYING YES AND THEN FIGURING IT OUT.**

On the day of the show, Ray asked me to voice the tease. The tease is those few sentences over exciting action at the beginning of a show that hooks the viewer on what is to come. It needs to be powerful and generate excitement. I read the script: "Tonight, the clash of crosstown rivals vying for the conference championship . . ."

As soon as I finished, Ray chastised me in front of the crew: "No! You need to have more emotion!" I read it again. He yelled, "That was worse! Do it again!" I exhaled and did it a third time with more animation in my voice. Exasperated, he said, "Ugh. You can't do this. I will have Bill voice the tease."

I hadn't met Bill before. He was a well-respected and experienced play-by-play announcer in Southern California. Bill looked at me and, holding down the mute button so no one could hear us, he said, "You can't win." Huh? At first, I thought he was trying to shake my confidence. But he repeated, "You can't win. Ray will never let you win. He set that up so he could say you suck. It actually has nothing to do with the way you voiced the tease. He just wanted to flex his muscles and knock you down." I understood. The man who took delight in being an ass when I interviewed and then turned me down time and time again now needed to make sure I knew I wasn't good enough. He had overpraised me after the sideline gig to set up the opportunity to knock me down again and act as if it was a mistake to hire me.

Bolstered by Bill's encouragement, I confidently sat at the anchor desk as the show started. When we reached the first commercial break, Ray barged up to the set. I rose out of my chair, greeting him with a smile and feeling excited about my work and proud of myself for figuring it out. "You are boring," he said.

Did the smile fall off my face, or was it frozen? "Excuse me?"

"You are BORING me!" he said louder so everyone could hear. "You are so slow. You are putting the audience to sleep!"

Thanks to Bill tipping me off, I knew that although Ray may have been right, he was also trying to rattle me. There was no constructive criticism there, just a straight up *you suck*. I realized Ray knew

I wasn't intimidated by him, *and he didn't like it.* He wanted to be feared, but I wasn't going to give that to him.

"Ok, Ray, are you ready?" He glared at me with a sneer. "Are you ready for me to have more energy? I am going to level it up right now. You'll see." And I flashed a wide, happy grin at him before walking back to the set. I knew it would it frustrate him to see I wasn't rattled. The camera's tally light turned red again, and I began speaking.

Now, let's be honest. Maybe you want me to write, "I knocked his socks off! He said I was amazing and hired me for the next year," but I had no idea how Ray felt, nor did I care. I was happy that I didn't back down in the face of criticism. I measured my performance by my own standards and effort. I was proud that I recalibrated my relationship with rejection. It was no longer something I feared, especially after I intentionally sought it out with Ray. In an audacious mindset, we conceive and conceptualize audacious moves. When we begin to take action, we graduate to level two in cultivating audacity—audacious behavior. The jump from dream to action is worth celebrating.

## Only Your Vote Counts

In her 2019 book *Limitless*, author Laura Gassner Otting wrote, "Don't give a vote to anyone who shouldn't have a voice."[2] Ray was my supervisor. He absolutely had every right to a voice in my performance, but I knew that validation from him wasn't going to happen. I decided Ray didn't deserve a vote.

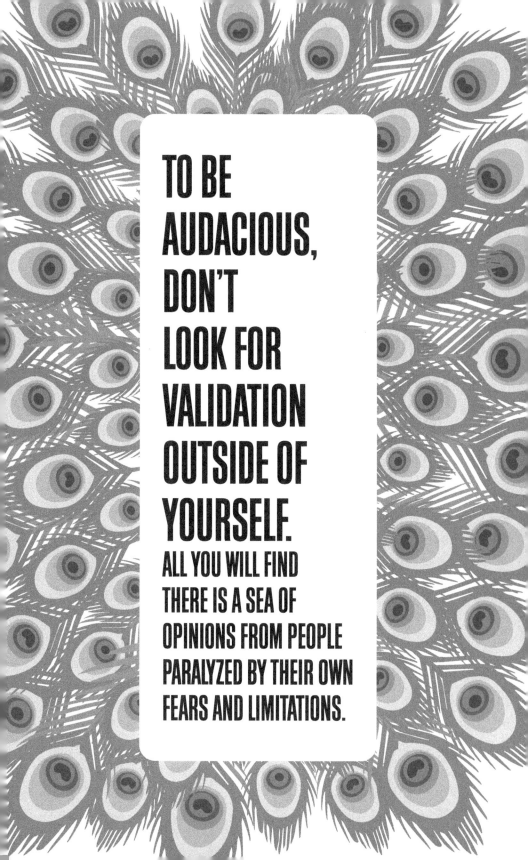

TO BE AUDACIOUS, DON'T LOOK FOR VALIDATION OUTSIDE OF YOURSELF. ALL YOU WILL FIND THERE IS A SEA OF OPINIONS FROM PEOPLE PARALYZED BY THEIR OWN FEARS AND LIMITATIONS.

To be audacious, don't look for validation outside of yourself. All you will find there is a sea of opinions from people paralyzed by their own fears and limitations. Their experiences color their world, so measuring your progress by their standards will never get you where you want to be. The only person for whom you should be making this change is YOU!

**RESENTMENT DOESN'T HAVE A HOME WHEN YOUR MOTIVATIONS COME FROM WITHIN.**

Seeking external approval for your decisions can only lead to resentment. If you change your work situation because someone else judges you for not spending enough time with your kids, then you may very well end up not only resenting that person but your children too. However, if you change your work hours because *you* want more time with family, the perspective is entirely different, though the change looks the same. That change isn't *for* that person or the kids—it is for *you*. Resentment doesn't have a home when your motivations come from within, even if the change benefits others.

## Just Try: From No to Not Yet

In 2018, a production company offered me a job as a play-by-play announcer for a professional women's basketball team. The season fit perfectly into my calendar, so I accepted and awaited the contract.

I kept waiting for over a month. A few weeks before the season, I checked in with the man who hired me. "Is everything ok? Contract on the way?"

He responded, "There is a problem. The general manager and head coach of the team has decided to hire someone else. I'm sorry."

I was livid. I'd never met the general manager/coach because the production company had hired me, but I had cleared my calendar for the summer work. Now that work was disappearing without me even meeting the man who decided he didn't want me. HELLLLLL NOOOO. I told the production company to let the team's headquarters know I was coming. I wanted to meet the man in charge.

I cry when I'm frustrated. My kids saw me angry with tears as I walked out of my house, drove to the airport, bought a ticket at the counter, and boarded the short flight. Upon landing, I took an Uber to the team's offices.

When I arrived, the head coach, who obviously didn't want to meet with me, said, "Look, this isn't personal."

"Of course it is. I am a person. I was told I had the job. What happened?"

He led me to his office, explaining he wanted to hire his friend. "I trust him," he said, which is completely reasonable.

I knew his friend was a white man in his 60s, so I asked, "Is that the person you think will best connect with your audience largely made up of women with a large LGBTQ+ fan base?" He was quiet. My intention was not to back him into a corner, so I asked a different question: "You just drafted the top post in the country, but you don't have anyone to pass inside to her. What is your plan?"

He told me about a point guard he'd just drafted. I knew the player and said, "She has had three ACL surgeries. It took her six years to finish her college eligibility because of injuries. You are banking on her to be the quarterback of your offense the entire season? What is the plan if she gets hurt again?"

I'm sure he was mildly annoyed that I was challenging him, but he knew it was a valid question. As a response, he asked one of his own. "Did you cover so and so in college?" I had. "Can she play defense?" He had another point guard in mind. I had called her games since her freshman year of college.

We went back and forth talking about personnel and his goals for the team for a while. Finally, he said, "Look, you know your stuff. I need some time to think about this, and we will get back to you."

I knew if I left that office at that moment, I wouldn't get the job. I'd flown there and introduced myself but still hadn't addressed his reluctance. I took an audacious risk, saying, "Let me make this easy for you. I don't want to work for you. I don't. Not if every time I walk into the gym, you roll your eyes and think, 'Oh, here is the *girl* I didn't want to hire.' But I will tell you this. I'm not a child. I have been a broadcaster for nearly 30 years. I flew here because I wanted you to meet the person you decided not to hire. Please don't give me the job because someone else says you should. I'm only accepting this job if you want me in that chair because I don't want to spend my summer looking over my shoulder."

And with that, I took an Uber back to the airport and flew home. By the time I arrived, he had called the production company and hired me—but first, he gave my starting salary a bump. The producer told me that he'd said, "I like her; she has balls and knows basketball."

It wasn't my words as much as my actions that got me hired. They said "No," and I heard "Not yet." The fear of rejection is never easy to deal with, and it might sound crazy, but shoot for the stars and fall short—early and often. Sometimes the no you hear can turn into a not yet, and other times it means "next." But shifting to a not yet or next requires garnering the gumption to challenge the no. It requires the audacity to just try.

## Catastrophize Your Life

Having a relationship with fear can be revelatory. We spend so much time pushing it away that fear plays an antagonist role in our lives. Once you tap into it and explore what is at the root of your trepidation, it is far less likely to spiral. Create a story in which everything you dread materializes, pointing to an irrational end. Catastrophize your worry to a ridiculous level rather than shrinking from it.

> **INTENTIONALLY EXAGGERATE AND TAKE YOUR FEAR TO A RIDICULOUS LEVEL RATHER THAN LETTING IT DRAG YOU UNDER.**

My exaggerated fear story could be, "If I go on air and am bad, which I certainly will be because I haven't done it before, then everyone will see me, and I will be embarrassed. If I am embarrassed, I will always be afraid to be in front of the camera, and then I certainly won't get better and will lose my job on air. The reporters for whom I produce won't take my advice once they see I can't do their job, so I will lose that job too. Jobless and humiliated, I will become depressed and difficult to live with, forcing my husband to leave me and take the kids because I won't be a good mother. Without a job or family, I will die destitute and alone." Whew, that's a lot! But that is what I mean when I say catastrophize your fear. Lay out every possible thing that could go wrong as a result of taking the risk. When dying destitute and alone is the feared outcome, anything short of that is a success, right?

Once you write the fear story all the way to the end, it will become clear that it is absolutely absurd! It's simply never going to happen. Now picture the very best that could happen and the very worst. Your outcome will most certainly lie in the middle. I now count fear among my friends because it is an essential barometer in my life. I use fear as a scale when considering whether a move is reckless or worth it.

Remember, fear is designed to keep us safe. If you aren't at least a little bit afraid, maybe you aren't pursuing a goal that will move you forward. As Amelia Earhart once said, "Use your fear, it can take you to the place where you store your courage."

## Redefining Fear and Failure

As you begin to get comfortable with the idea of exploring fear, consider defining what failure means to you. What is failure in your situation exactly? Is it a failure if you learn from it? Let's say you put a new marketing plan in place for your consulting business, and your revenue doesn't increase. Is that failure? Or is that data pointing you toward a different plan that could be more lucrative? Recognize how each setback in your life has contributed to your personal development.

**USE YOUR FEAR, IT CAN TAKE YOU TO THE PLACE WHERE YOU STORE YOUR COURAGE.**

**— AMELIA EARHART**

For example, I like to look back on jobs I didn't get and jobs I lost as detours leading to growth. It all is just data that fed my personal development. Failure is not trying. That is my definition of failure: not even trying.

Embracing failure as a stepping stone to success transforms fear into a valuable teacher, but you have to understand it first. Use the prompts below to uncover the details about your fear:

**Paralysis Analysis:** Reflect on past instances where fear held you back. What opportunities were missed due to fear?

**Fear Identification:** Identify and name the specific fears hindering your audacious journey. This can include but is not limited to the fear of failure, fear of judgment, fear of the unknown, fear of rejection, or fear of embarrassment.

**Fear's Root Cause:** Explore the underlying reasons for your specific fears. Recognize that they often stem from self-doubt, past experiences, or societal pressures.

**Fear's Cost:** Consider the cost of allowing fear to dictate your choices. If you don't take the leap, you are denying yourself an opportunity for growth. Remember FOSS—the fear of staying the same? Does the pain of your current circumstances outweigh your fear of the unknown?

Once you have a better understanding of the role fear has played in your past, reflect on how your relationship with fear can shift to enhance rather than hinder your audacious future. These tools will help:

**Fear Journal:** Keep a journal to document your fears, their triggers, and the emotions associated with them.

**Fear Visualization:** Spend time envisioning yourself overcoming your fears successfully. Focus less on the end result and more on the audacity of your effort despite the discomfort. Remember, the brain believes what you tell it.

**Fear Exposure Challenges:** Develop a series of exposure challenges tailored to each fear, starting with the least intimidating.

**Failure Celebration:** (I know, I'm quirky, but this works!) Reflect on the lessons you've learned from past failures and celebrate them as creators guiding you toward your goals.

When changing your relationship with fear, you'll start to view it as a map—keeping you on the right path and helping you separate the worth it from the reckless risks. Fear can fuel your growth if you don't let it paralyze you from taking bold risks. Once you make friends with fear, be prepared for another barrier to arise. It will most likely be time. "I'm not afraid to do it, but I'm so busy I just don't have time." That is just another desperate attempt by your superego to protect you from hurt or disappointment. Your superego is not a fan of going out on a limb. There is time. I promise. Let's dive into it. Turn the page.

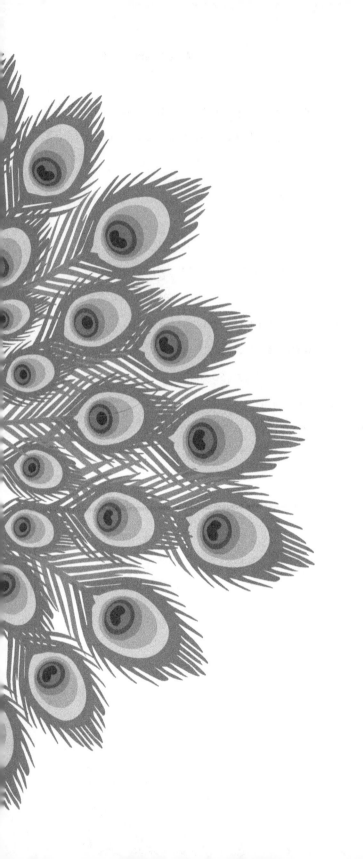

# 5

# THE URGENCY FALLACY

When I started keynote speaking, I knew I needed to dedicate at least an hour each day to prospecting and connecting with potential clients. I used that hour to contact event planners, draw up contracts, write speeches, and make travel arrangements. I still had my daily tasks (wake, feed, and get the kids out the door on time for school, prepare my television games, run the household, etc.), but I promised myself to prioritize speaking. So, I set my daily alarm for 4:30 a.m. to get an hour devoted to keynotes in before the kids woke up.

It worked great. My speaking business gained momentum, and more money flowed in. You know what else? *It sucked.* I had accomplished my goal of booking more events but was exhausted by the time afternoon came around. If I had a game to call on television at night, I wouldn't get home until 11:30 or midnight. It didn't take long for the 4:30 a.m. wake-up calls to become untenable. I needed a daily hour of prospecting to build my business, but the before-dawn mornings were wearing me down. I needed a new plan.

It is easy to get caught in a perpetual whirlpool of busyness. I felt barraged daily by emails, phone calls, meetings, creating contracts, school pickups, television preparation, running the house, and an endless list of "must-do" tasks. It can feel selfish to prioritize building an audacious life before everything else gets done.

**EVERY HOUR ISN'T EQUAL IN VALUE.**

"I don't have time!" is the common cry, and there is truth in it for each of us. No one has excess time. But when we say it like that—"I don't have time!"—we treat all time the same, as if every hour were equal in value. Yet every hour isn't equal, nor does it require the same amount of energy or yield results that provide similar value. The level of concentration and focus required to exercise versus starting a new business varies dramatically.

## The Urgency Fallacy: Urgent Versus Important

Often, we prioritize tasks that provide the short-term satisfaction of checking items off our to-do lists while neglecting the work we need to do to create long-term happiness. The fallacy is our belief that activities demanding immediate attention are the most important and should take priority over all else. If you want to make an audacious change in your life, you must distinguish between *urgent* and *important* duties and block out time for the work that points toward where you want to go. If you don't, the endless to-do list takes over, and you find yourself on the hamster wheel day after day.

Let's break down the difference between urgent and important tasks.

### Urgent tasks
- Have a pressing deadline.
- Tend to be reactive in nature, often triggered by external factors.
- Can be completed quickly and provide a sense of immediate accomplishment.

### Important tasks
- Contribute significantly to your long-term goals, values, and vision.
- May not have an impending deadline but have substantial consequences if neglected.
- Typically require more time, effort, and strategic planning.

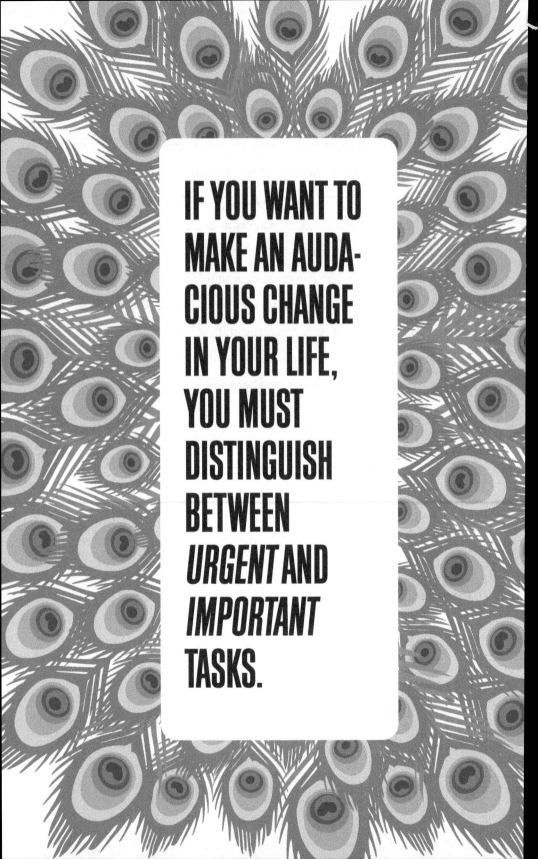

IF YOU WANT TO MAKE AN AUDA-CIOUS CHANGE IN YOUR LIFE, YOU MUST DISTINGUISH BETWEEN *URGENT* AND *IMPORTANT* TASKS.

It is natural to prioritize an urgent task over an important one, but urgent tasks will always get done. By definition, urgent duties must be completed even if we don't labor over the details because we are racing the clock. Our audacious dreams are important to us, but they need to be handled with much more deliberation and care. Why haven't you already made your audacious move if it's so important? Because we push aside the work to make it happen until we "have time."

As a sidenote, let's be clear: Urgent and emergency are different. Almost anything urgent can wait 15 minutes. Your child bleeding out on the floor is not urgent—that is an emergency! Of course, emergencies come first! Your child asking you to make them a snack is not an emergency. The request by your boss to respond to an email is not an emergency. It needs to be done, and it needs to be done soon, but it is not an emergency.

Important tasks must be prioritized above the urgent ones. Why? Because if you handle what's urgent first, then by the time you get to what is important, it might be late in the day or the week or the month—and it gets put off until the "right time." The same cannot be said for anything urgent because it is already attached to a deadline—that's why it's urgent. I will pay the bills, answer that email, help with homework, feed the kids, and sign the permission slip. But if I did those things first, I might not get an hour in to work out, build my business, or prospect speaking events and be tempted to push it off until tomorrow, when maybe things won't be so busy.

We all know that is a lie. Tomorrow will be busy and could be even more packed. The adage says, "Don't put off until tomorrow what you can do today." Tomorrow, there could be an emergency. I should have named my middle son "Co-Pay" for all the times he has needed a trip to the ER. If he isn't bleeding, my level of concern drops from emergency to optional in less than five seconds. I can answer emails in the emergency room. I cannot call a client or write a book. When budgeting your time, create space for what's important first.

Can your urgent thing wait 15 minutes while you prioritize what's important?

## A Case Study in How to Find Time and Eliminate Barriers

Recently, I decided to treat myself to a massage. I asked the practitioner, Tammy, if she enjoyed being a masseuse. She hesitated and said, "I like it, I guess." That didn't sound like she was living her best life.

"What do you enjoy doing?" I asked.

Tammy didn't hesitate. "I love to organize." I asked if she thought she was good at organizing: "Oh yes, I'm very good, and my friends often ask me to help them organize their homes."

After reading chapter 2, you know exactly where I was going with my questions. I was looking for her ikigai. Tammy shared how she found satisfaction in helping her friends have more efficient homes and enjoyed seeing everything labeled and having its own space. She also felt valued. "It makes me so happy when I get a call a week or two later telling me how much better their life is because they have a neat and organized space." Clearly, that passed right through all the checkpoints in the Freedom Funnel. She enjoyed organizing and was good at it. The world needs organization, and people will pay for help accomplishing it. Work as an organizer should be in her bucket at the base of that exercise.

## CAN YOUR URGENT THING WAIT 15 MINUTES WHILE YOU PRIORITIZE WHAT'S IMPORTANT?

When I suggested she start an organization business, she sighed, "I don't have time."

As our conversation continued, I began to understand. Tammy's father had passed away two and half years prior. He had run the family restaurant that has been a centerpiece in our little beach town for decades. No one else in Tammy's family wanted to take it over, so she assumed responsibility, telling me she didn't want to let down the wonderful employees who built their lives around employment there. "It just feels wrong to close it. It feels like I would be letting the entire town down." That's heavy.

She also told me that when her dad died, she took over running the family property management business. "I am the only one in my family that can do it," she explained. "I don't love it, but I'm decent at it." Three jobs and the significant and real burden of not wanting to let others down is a very good explanation of why Tammy didn't think she had time to make an audacious move creating a home organization business.

But it also didn't feel right that Tammy, who was in her late 40s, would spend the rest of her life working three jobs that served others, but none of which motivated her to get up every day. We needed to create time for Tammy without ignoring her responsibilities or having her income drop.

Her calendar was full of daily urgent tasks: the operations of the restaurant, keeping up with the new, ever-changing laws, running payroll for both businesses, and managing her home. Although she is a terrific masseuse, I focused my attention there.

"What if," I asked her, "you cut one day of massage and replaced it with organizing for clients?"

Immediately, her barriers lined up and the questions came pouring out. "What if no one wants me to organize for them? When could I possibly fit that in? I can't take time away from any of my jobs—I need the money. I have no idea how to even start! How would I get clients? I don't have any special qualifications to make me an organizer."

We went through each barrier one at a time.

### "What if no one wants me to organize for them?"

That is the fear of rejection. If Tammy were to offer her services and no one wanted them, it might confirm that she wasn't meant to organize, and it would be disappointing and embarrassing not to have clients. I assured her if no one wanted her organizing services one week, she could open that spot up again for massage clients. She was absolutely in demand as a massage therapist. I was always on her waiting list and rarely got in without an appointment made weeks in advance.

**"When could I possibly fit that in?"**

Time and the urgency fallacy were taking hold. Some of Tammy's jobs were undoubtedly urgent. The restaurant and property management were both going to stay on her plate. But if she took fewer massage clients, she would have some potential windows to work on what was important to her—in this case, a home organization business.

**"I can't cut massage clients because I need the money."**

Tammy charged $65 an hour for a massage. I proposed that she charge $90 an hour for her organizing services. It would be an ever-so-slight bump in her hourly rate, allowing her to make the same or a little more money in the same amount of time. I also knew that people in our area paid as much as $150 an hour for organization services, so the potential to up her income was significant by building a client base and resume with a more consumer-friendly price point.

**"I have no idea how to even start! How would I get clients?"**

I suggested she tell people about it: her friends, her massage clients, put it on Instagram, and post it on the message board at her restaurant. She didn't need a huge number of clients; she just needed to get started.

"I don't have any special qualifications to make me an organizer." There it is . . . "I'm not ready." Go all the way back to chapter 1 and stop waiting until you have all the qualifications you think you need. There was Tammy on the sticky floor, waiting for the right moment. The longer we wait, the more deeply entrenched

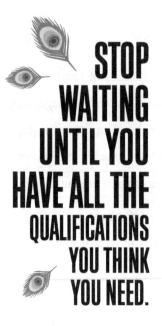

**STOP WAITING UNTIL YOU HAVE ALL THE QUALIFICATIONS YOU THINK YOU NEED.**

we become on a path we happened upon by accident rather than one we consciously choose.

## Audit Your Time

The work that needs to be done to create an audacious life, while important, doesn't necessarily have to be done right this minute. How do you create that space when you are deep in the weeds, trying to keep everything urgent around you afloat?

Before you can manage your time, you must know what you do with it. You may have sat at your desk for six hours today, but were you working all six of those hours? Or did you take a little time to scroll social media? Maybe (God willing) you have this book in your bag and pulled it out for inspiration? Lunch? A stroll? Pick up your dry cleaning?

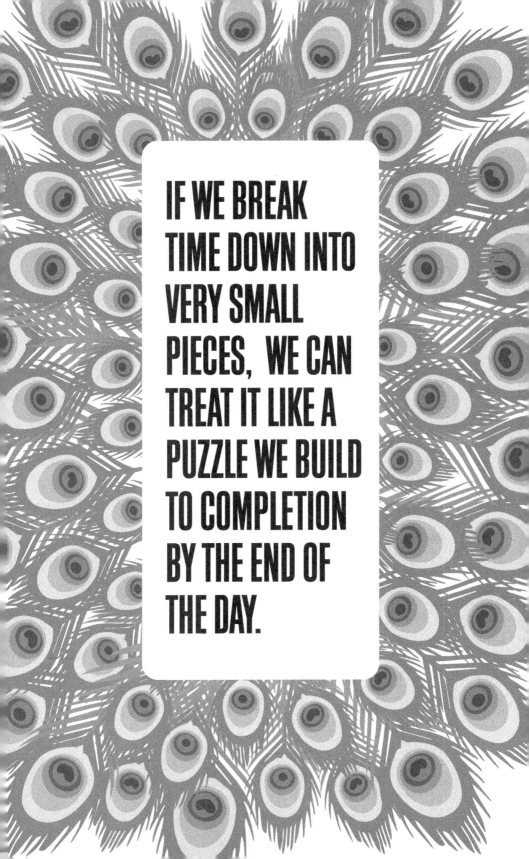

IF WE BREAK
TIME DOWN INTO
VERY SMALL
PIECES, WE CAN
TREAT IT LIKE A
PUZZLE WE BUILD
TO COMPLETION
BY THE END OF
THE DAY.

Begin with a time audit. How do you really spend your time? Keep a log each day for a week. Act as a social scientist, noting not just the

labor but how you feel about it as well. Which times stress you out? Bring you joy? Energize you? Make it as detailed as possible, including the time spent on your morning routine, commute, work, sleep, eating, scrolling, socializing, hobbies, chores, and anything else you do during your waking hours.

Once you have collected a week's worth of data, put it into a chart so you have a visual representation of how you spend your days. I like a pie chart, but others prefer a graph.

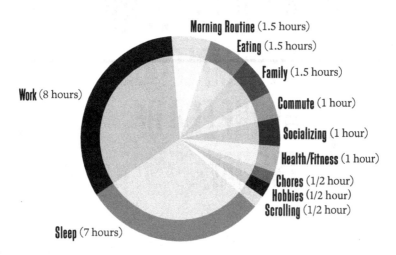

As you look at the visual representation of your time, reflect on your current commitments and evaluate if some can be adjusted or eliminated to hold space for the life you are creating. Identify common time-wasting activities or habits that divert your focus from what is important.

Time is finite, so it is up to us to budget our time in alignment with our goals. If you want to improve your fitness, more time allocated to exercise, nutrition, and recovery is appropriate. If your focus is starting an online coaching business, devoting time to promoting your services on social media is necessary. It may be possible to double up activities for tasks that require less focus and intensity. For example, if you go for a walk, perhaps return calls simultaneously. If you need to brainstorm potential donors for a fundraiser, you could record your ideas as voice notes while taking care of laundry or other routine chores in your home. If we break time down into very small pieces, we can treat it like a puzzle we build to completion by the end of the day.

Once you have visually charted your days and week, create one more category—your audacious dream—and assess how you can shave slivers of time from other areas to reallocate toward your goal. It is only after you know how you have been spending your time that you can begin to create space for the move you want to make. It doesn't need to occupy a large percentage of the pie, but it needs to have a place. Visually, your mind will not allow you to have a category with a zero percentage. Just by seeing it on your chart, you will begin to fill it.

**TIME FOR YOUR AUDACIOUS WORK DOESN'T NEED TO OCCUPY A LARGE PERCENTAGE OF THE PIE, BUT IT NEEDS TO HAVE A PLACE.**

As you assess your time audit, consider if your pride is getting in the way. Are you so indispensable that you can't hand over some of your load to someone else and better use that window of opportunity? I have traveled for work throughout my 20 years as a mother. I had to let go of controlling what happens at home when I am gone. Once, after returning from a week-long business trip, I woke my then three-year-old and told him it was time for breakfast. He threw his hands in the air enthusiastically and said, "PIZZA!" I didn't find it funny but decided to bite my tongue (not easy for me!). I had to let that go and allow my kids' father to parent in peace without me looking over his shoulder. When you take your pride out of the decision-making process, it becomes easier to streamline your vision.

## The Time Block Method

For years, my friend Brian told me he wanted to get his real estate license. He just needed time to properly study, and when he felt adequately prepared, he would take the test. But, with his job and a young family, Brian had difficulty finding study time.

Fear is often the first obstacle between us and our audacious journey, so that has to be addressed. I asked what he was afraid of, and he said, "I'm afraid to fail." I suggested he do exactly that *first*: Go fail the test. He looked at me like I was crazy. "Fail on purpose?" Not exactly. I encouraged him to try his best, but since he wasn't prepared, I surmised that would be the likely outcome. When failing didn't kill him, I explained, he could then move on to confronting his time barrier.

There isn't a limit on how many times one can take the real estate test. It was $60 per attempt, so retaking it wouldn't hurt Brian financially, but it would free him of that fear. The worst that could happen in his mind—failing—happened, and he survived. Failing

WHEN YOU TAKE YOUR PRIDE OUT OF THE DECISION-MAKING PROCESS, IT BECOMES EASIER TO STREAMLINE YOUR VISION.

was Brian's first barrier. His next obstacle was time, but only after he made friends with fear could he begin creating a study habit.

After charting his time, Brian decided on half-hour study blocks twice a day. The first was early in the morning, immediately after checking his email before his family woke up. His second block was in the evening before reading to his young daughters. He enlisted his wife to help with his study plan, and they agreed that while he was trying to pass the test, she would handle bath time for both girls, freeing up that half hour for his studying. In his toddlers' evening routine, he helped his wife get the girls into the bath and then locked himself away to study for 30 minutes, returning in time to read to them and tuck the girls in bed. After studying for another month, Brian tried again and failed a second time before passing on his third attempt. Having tackled the two barriers standing between him and the life he wanted, Brian got his license.

For my keynote speaking business, I eventually landed on 15-minute blocks throughout the day to save myself from those grueling early mornings, and I used the same time block method to write this book. Sometimes, I could only spare 15 minutes before I needed to return to my urgent tasks. Four times a day, I'd hear my phone alarm ringing, reminding me to take 15 or 20 minutes to write. Locking myself in the bathroom (the best place for some peace and quiet), I'd sit on the floor and type out the words that became this book.

Writing this book, I decided, was important. It brought me closer to my overarching goal—helping you figure out what is important to you and how to live the life you want.

Important tasks align with your long-term objectives, helping you move closer to your aspirations and dreams. Focusing on urgency can lead to a reactive approach, pulling you away from your desired path. I am not suggesting you shove urgent duties aside indefi-nitely—that would be reckless. Part of creating an audacious life is delineating between what puts you in a precarious position and what advances your goals. So do your urgent tasks, but before you tackle that looming deadline, carve out a nonnegotiable window to work on what is important to you.

Your time budget isn't the only budget you need to cultivate audacity. Time and money are deeply connected. Benjamin Franklin coined the phrase "time is money,"[3] and indeed, they are in many ways interchangeable. Both must be budgeted. Consider them twins, as your relationship with one will almost always mirror the other. The approach to them is similar: Evaluate how much you have of each and then distribute accordingly. You have taken a close look at how you spend time. Now, examine your relationship with money. Turn the page.

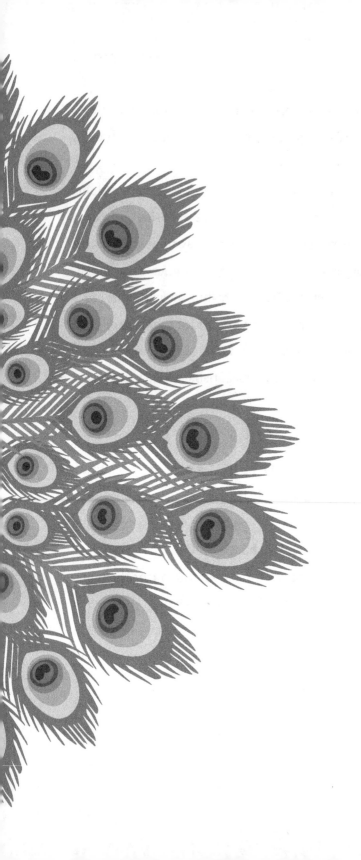

CHAPTER

# MONEY: TIME'S TWIN

Many people think you don't deserve to make money if you aren't working your tail off. If you don't bust your butt, the story becomes "you don't deserve it." The grind is your identity. That was me.

There have been times in my adult life when I've had three jobs. When transitioning to reporting at ESPN, I was still producing during the week and sideline reporting on the weekend. At the same time, I was writing freelance pieces for *ESPN The Magazine*. I never had any time off working seven days a week . . . and I was proud of that. I thought being a grinder all day, every day, was something to be admired.

At the height of my more-is-better frenzy, I was calling nearly 100 live events a year. That's insane! In 2009, I was in Fox's studios anchoring news breaks while also calling games as a play-by-play announcer for four different sports on ESPN with two toddlers at home and one more to come. I will never forget the day one of my colleagues looked at me and asked, "Why do you work so hard?" I was confused by the question. What did he mean? Don't we all work hard and hustle? Isn't that what we are supposed to do? To be honest, I was insulted, thinking he was judging my time away from the kids (because that is what I felt guilty about). The struggle zone was my comfort zone.

When I began writing this book, I knew I was adding a significant load to my schedule, which was already filled with calling games on live television and traveling the country as a keynote speaker. My oldest son had started his freshman year at a university two time zones away. In the spring of his senior year in high school, I missed a lot of milestone events. He told me it didn't matter to him that I wasn't there, but it mattered to me. I sat in a hotel lobby a world away in Türkiye, on assignment, watching his high school graduation on my laptop with tears running down my cheeks. I regret that decision.

When I returned home, I looked at my other two children, who were 15 and 11, and thought, *They are leaving soon too. I need more time with them.* I needed to reevaluate how I was spending my time. I adjusted the way I made decisions about which assignments to accept, no longer prioritizing offers from the biggest networks or the ones that paid the most. I decided to only take games close to home so if plane travel was involved, I could be on a crack-of-dawn early flight the morning after the event, often arriving home in time to take the kids to school. Over the course of a few years, I dropped my workload from 96 to 50 live events a year. Did my income drop? Of course, but only for a short time. With the reallocation of my time, I began booking more speaking engagements, for which I earned more per event than per television game, so my income rose even while cutting back travel and work hours.

**MONEY IS TIME'S TWIN BECAUSE THE APPROACH TO OVERCOMING TIME AND MONEY BARRIERS IS SIMILAR.**

That would have never happened if I hadn't been willing to look at my finances, evaluate the risk, and commit to making the change.

I refer to money as time's twin because the approach to overcoming time and money barriers is similar. In the last chapter, we kept track of how we spent our time and then created a new way to prioritize by emphasizing what is important over urgent. Most often, our relationship with money and time mirror each other. Those who struggle to budget their time also struggle to budget their money. We need to get clear about how much money we have before we can begin making decisions about how to allocate it wisely.

This chapter is about the role money plays as you consider the support necessary to follow your audacious path. According to a 2023 Capital One study, 73 percent of Americans rank finances as the number one stressor in their lives.[4] It is a reckless risk to quit your current job to pursue your passion and purpose without first taking a deep dive into your current financial situation. The only way to do that is to explore your money story. We all have a relationship with money that goes back to when we were children, and we must unearth our most basic feelings about money before overcoming this barrier.

## What's Your Money Story?

Think back to when you were growing up. What were the discussions about money like in your household? Were they easygoing and open, or did they feel a bit tense and hush-hush? Did your family lean toward saving and being careful with money, or were they more about enjoying the finer things and spending freely? What you came from is what you know. Once you dig into the roots of your ideas about money, you can start shaking up any old habits that aren't doing you any favors. That's when you can clear the path and make room for all the good stuff you dream of achieving.

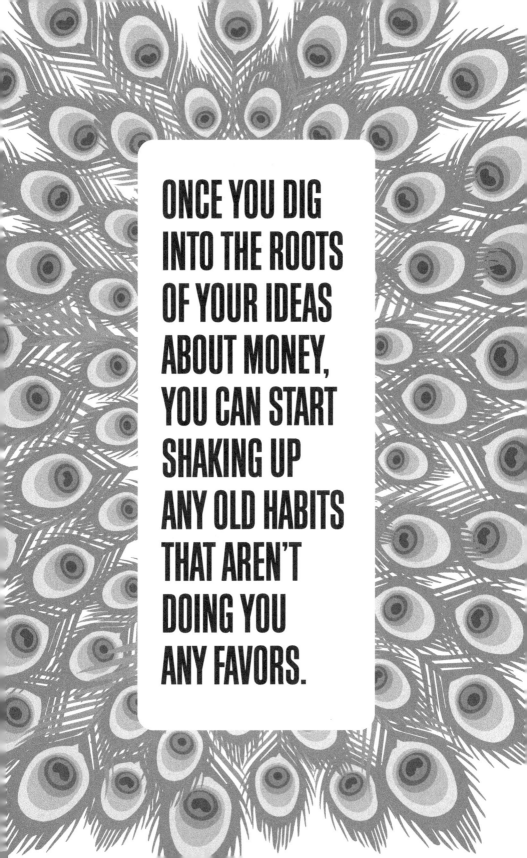

ONCE YOU DIG
INTO THE ROOTS
OF YOUR IDEAS
ABOUT MONEY,
YOU CAN START
SHAKING UP
ANY OLD HABITS
THAT AREN'T
DOING YOU
ANY FAVORS.

I grew up with parents who were very good about making wise decisions when choosing how to spend and save. They didn't buy a lot of toys or gifts. We didn't go out to eat often or wear fancy clothes. My mother taught me how to balance a checkbook. I never heard my parents fight about finances. As a result, my four brothers and I are all comfortable working with and budgeting our money. As I reflect on my childhood, growing up with a healthy attitude toward money may be one of the greatest gifts my parents gave our family.

Exploring what your family's relationship with money was like when you were a child is a journey of self-discovery that can yield valuable insights into your own financial mindset and behaviors. Many of us have an emotional association with money depending on the dynamics of our family patterns. If finances were a source of stress when you were young, you might feel the urge to stick your head in the sand rather than face the discomfort of your revelations. If you witnessed fighting followed by expensive gifts to make amends between your parents, you may associate money as a method of righting wrongs. Or perhaps you grew up in a home where your family was excessively frugal despite having enough money to live more comfortably; you may swing to the opposite end of the pendulum and spend lavishly and above your means.

Some people are so uncomfortable thinking and talking about finances that they would rather avoid it altogether. If you have a tenuous relationship with money because of a chaotic upbringing, please know it is not your fault. I am proud of you for reading this chapter and being willing to dive in. Your audacious goal cannot happen without this step.

## Evaluate Your Money Story

I reached out to Maryalice Goldsmith, a life coach who helps people build online businesses. Maryalice's first step in working with her clients is to evaluate their financial backstory, so I hoped she would help by sharing her approach. My creativity came to a screeching halt when it came time to write on this subject. She asked about my attitude toward money. I didn't think I had *any* attitude related to it; I just don't get too excited one way or the other. We chatted about our childhoods, parenting, and business. After a few minutes, she said, "Notice how your relationship with time and money are similar. You don't lament it; you just distribute it in alignment with your goals because that is what you saw growing up." The word *lament* resonated with me. It is true: I don't have any anxiety, angst, or emotion attached to money. Whether I make a lot of money on an assignment or earn below my going rate, it doesn't affect me emotionally.

Maryalice's story was very different. "I used to avoid money because I didn't grow up in a situation similar to yours." As the youngest of seven, her family had enough money for their basic needs but definitely not an abundance. There was an unspoken understanding that the men in her family could spend as they pleased, but the women needed to seek permission. When Maryalice became an adult, she didn't feel financially worthy because she had a hard time asking her father for money growing up. When he did give it, he would grudgingly say, "Why should I give you money so you can go to the movies? How does that benefit me?"

Bingo! That is her money story!

"When I decided I wanted to take my business from five figures to six, I knew I couldn't stick my head in the sand about money any longer," she explained. Maryalice confessed that prior to building her business, she rarely looked at her bank balance. Just the thought of seeing her account balance stressed her out.

The first step in changing her money story was to incorporate looking at her bank account as part of her morning routine. Every morning, she would brush her teeth, comb her hair, and check her bank balance. "It didn't matter if there were thousands of dollars in there or ten dollars, I said, 'Thanks so much for being here.' I didn't judge the balance. I just thanked the money for being there."

I giggled, assuming she was being metaphorical until she explained, "I would literally say out loud, 'Thank you for being here,' and close the bank statement and move on with my day. If I hadn't done that, no way would my business have grown to multiple six figures. Not happening. I didn't need more clients. I needed to get right with my money. I created a spreadsheet, a budget, and started nurturing it. I looked at it every day."

That was a foreign concept to me, but I soon grasped why she asked about my attitude toward money—she had guilt and shame as emotional attachments to finances. Maryalice was more comfortable giving than receiving, so it felt wrong to be concerned with something as material as money. As a giver, she didn't feel worthy of it, and it felt *wrong* to want money.

"The more I allowed myself to desire the money, the more I allowed myself to make. I had to examine where I learned that I shouldn't make money. I am a nurturer, so I want to give and not take. I gave myself permission to live abundantly in every way by embracing the idea that if I made more money, then I would have more to give."

As you evaluate your story, take ownership. The money story constructed during childhood is not your fault, but it is your responsibility to examine it and write your own story. Blaming your current circumstance on your past isn't the answer. The hard truth is that where you are now is what you have allowed. The choices you have made as an adult have led you here. When you know better, you do better! The money story you grew up with isn't the story you need to continue. Don't focus on a low bank balance; instead, concentrate on growing what you already have. If you focus on the roots—financial health and clarity—the fruit will be amazing.

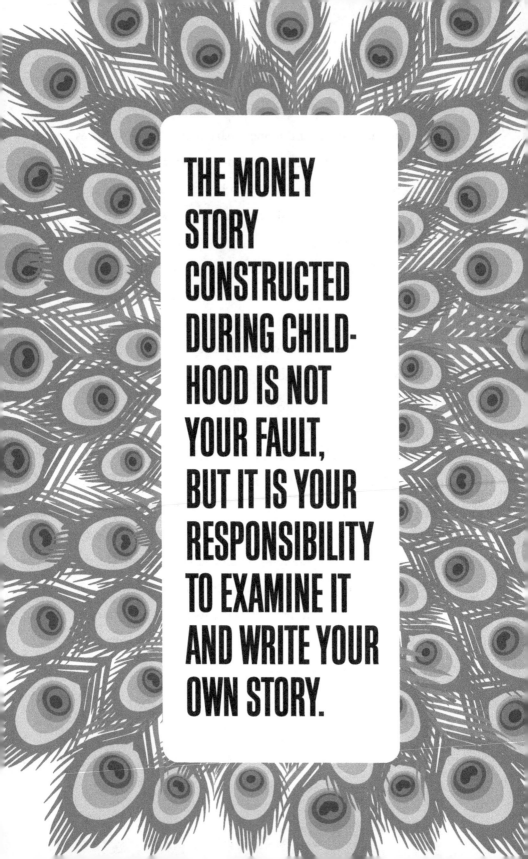

THE MONEY STORY CONSTRUCTED DURING CHILDHOOD IS NOT YOUR FAULT, BUT IT IS YOUR RESPONSIBILITY TO EXAMINE IT AND WRITE YOUR OWN STORY.

## Craft a New Money Story

Some people subconsciously need earning money to be hard and struggle to feel worthy of it, as I did. Tammy, the masseuse who wanted to be an organizer in the last chapter, identified time as her primary barrier, but money was closely related. She needed to be careful not to trade one barrier for another. Tammy expressed guilt about taking time away from the restaurant to pursue a career in organizing. She talked about the obligation she felt to continue employing the people who have worked in the restaurant for decades. She had been sacrificing and grinding her entire life, a feeling which only intensified after her father passed away. Tammy was so blinded by the heavy weight of her daily obligations that, at first, she couldn't even connect that trading a $65-an-hour massage for $90 to $150 per hour of organizing would bring in more money, not less.

We all need to make a conscious decision: Are we going to remain stagnant in our relationship with money, or are we willing to invest in deconstructing that story and building a new one?

You may need to break through some deep beliefs about wealth and give yourself permission to go down that road and ask, "What would my life look like if I allowed myself to have an abundance of wealth?" Perhaps you conflate abundance with greed. Take some time to wonder what it would look and feel like. Get comfortable with the feeling of, I do want a nice car. I want to travel. I want experiences. I want these things. We must be open to our deepest desires and not shove them back in the box, punishing ourselves with guilt. We need to allow ourselves to feel worthy. So many of us are apologetic about making money. "Oh gosh, I feel so bad that I am making money while my friend is broke." Shed that skin. We all make choices, and changing your money story and welcoming wealth isn't going to heal your friend's money story.

On the flip side, if we have overspent due to an overly lavish upbringing, that also needs some recalibration. Those questions are different. Why do I need this designer dress? Do I need an expensive car to commute more comfortably or to impress my friends? Delve into your feelings when you see someone in worn-out clothing or owning an older car or house less expensive than yours. Do you see them as "less than" because you felt less than when you grew up without those things?

My ex-husband and I grew up with very different money stories. I grew up comfortably but without excessive spending. Matt grew up on the free lunch program at school and with the worry his family wouldn't have enough money for basic needs. Three years into our marriage, we moved to Colorado. Our house was so hot one February day that I kept turning the heat down. Matt kept turning it back up. The cycle repeated until I finally said, "It is roasting in here. Why do you need the heat so high?"

Matt snapped at me, "We can afford heat, so we are gonna have heat!" I was surprised by his reaction. He went on to explain that growing up in New York, the heat in his home was turned off several times because of unpaid bills. He and his siblings were shivering in their childhood home, wearing their winter coats to bed. With that knowledge, I could better understand his behavior. Even though we had plenty of money to pay our heating bill, Matt still associated being cold with financial insecurity. Once he was aware of that childhood link, we were able to have a more moderately heated home.

## Choose the Story to Pass On

Since we inherit money stories, most people subconsciously adopt it as their story too. With your awareness, you now have a choice not just about your relationship with money but the messages you are passing along to your children.

When money becomes a source of stress and limitations, it can seep into every corner of our lives, casting a shadow of worry and tension. Parents who struggle to make ends meet or exhibit irresponsible financial behaviors, such as overspending or accumulating debt, inadvertently impart lessons in financial hardship and scarcity, shaping their children's attitudes toward money in profound ways.

One of the most stressful scenarios relating to money for a child is standing at the checkout counter, wondering if their parent's credit card will be denied. If you grew up hearing, "I hope this credit card works," as your parents approached the register, then the chances of you living the same way and passing that history on to your children are high. It is an inherited story in the same way that the little girl who hears her mother say, "I look so fat in this," will likely struggle with body image.

The thought of being frivolous with money has never entered my mind because I grew up respecting it, saving it, and managing it. I did, however, need to learn how to *spend* money. Sometimes, you have to spend money to buy back energy to make pursuing your dream achievable. Some people don't want to spend a penny and deny themselves the comforts that would help make pursuing their audacious quest easier or more satisfying.

## Money Is Energy

I travel widely as both a broadcaster and speaker. As I began writing this book, I couldn't keep up with many of the daily tasks that needed

THE ADAGE "TIME IS MONEY" CAN EVOLVE INTO "MONEY IS ENERGY."

to be done for both of my jobs, and as a result, I was spending less time with my children. Maryalice urged me to hire an assistant. It felt pretentious to hire an assistant, and I considered it an unnecessary luxury when I should save every dime for my children's college educations. I also wanted to keep a good stash for a rainy day.

Maryalice introduced me to a new way of thinking. The adage "time is money" can evolve into "money is energy." She urged me to view both time and money as commodities to be traded for whatever I needed to help me succeed. The hours I was putting into contracts, making business travel plans, and following up with speaking clients were impacting my ability to spend time writing. I was exhausted and didn't feel like I was giving my best to my jobs or family.

She helped me recognize that paying someone to help with paperwork was a form of prioritizing important tasks over the urgent, repetitive ones that consumed so much of my energy. At Maryalice's urging, I hired an operations manager for my business to take over the back-office tasks I didn't want to do. It was an exchange of energy. Having an assistant cost money (energy), but it also freed up

**SOMETIMES, YOU HAVE TO SPEND MONEY TO BUY BACK ENERGY TO MAKE PURSUING YOUR DREAM ACHIEVABLE.**

the time (also energy) to pursue my goals. Within six weeks of hiring my assistant, Fabi, I began booking more speaking events because I could prospect new clients rather than get bogged down in details and paperwork. The money I exchanged by paying Fabi correlated directly to an increase in my income.

Just as we discussed separating time into urgent and important categories, we can also put our money into buckets. Necessary expenses include the house items, bills, credit card, etc.—all your basic living standards and obligations. Don't put any of that on the back burner to pursue your audacious goals. In this case, urgent equates to necessary, and you must pay it. Anything else would be reckless. The other category is discretionary income. You may need to redistribute your discretionary income after paying for basic needs and bills.

Don't go clutching your coffee money just yet. That is what people always go for first, isn't it? A trip to Starbucks can indeed have a steep price. The exchange of energy needs to balance long-term planning with present enjoyment. If your morning cup of joe gives you pleasure, then by all means, have it. Look for other areas in your discretionary bucket to adjust.

## Track Your Spending

In chapter 5 we logged our time. Tracking your spending is a crucial first step in this process, providing valuable insights into your habits, patterns, and priorities. Whether you prefer traditional pen and paper, spreadsheets, or specialized budgeting apps, the key is to select a method that aligns with your preferences and lifestyle.

Next, categorize your expenses into broad categories such as housing, transportation, food, utilities, entertainment, and miscellaneous. Within each category, create subcategories to further break down your spending. For example, under the food category, you might have subcategories like groceries, dining out, and coffee. Tailor your categories to reflect your specific spending habits and priorities, ensuring comprehensive coverage of your expenses.

Gather all relevant financial documents, including bank statements, credit card statements, receipts, and bills. Review these documents to identify and categorize your expenses accurately. I'll be honest: This is the step where I stall and procrastinate. I don't enjoy that kind of detailed work, but it is important to capture all transactions. Be thorough and meticulous in your approach, no matter how small or insignificant the expenses seem.

## ARE YOU SUFFICIENTLY FUNDING YOUR AUDACIOUS GOALS AND THE THINGS THAT ARE IMPORTANT TO YOU?

Record each transaction as it occurs, noting the date, amount, and category/subcategory. Be diligent and consistent in your tracking efforts, making it a daily or weekly habit to update your records. Consider setting reminders or alerts to prompt you to track your spending regularly.

Once it is all charted, look for trends, fluctuations, and areas where you may be overspending or underspending. Identify areas for adjustment. Are you sufficiently funding your audacious goals and the things that are important to you? In which categories are there opportunities for optimization and improvement, such as reducing discretionary expenses or renegotiating recurring bills?

Allocate resources toward your priorities and goals while also ensuring that you maintain a balanced and sustainable approach

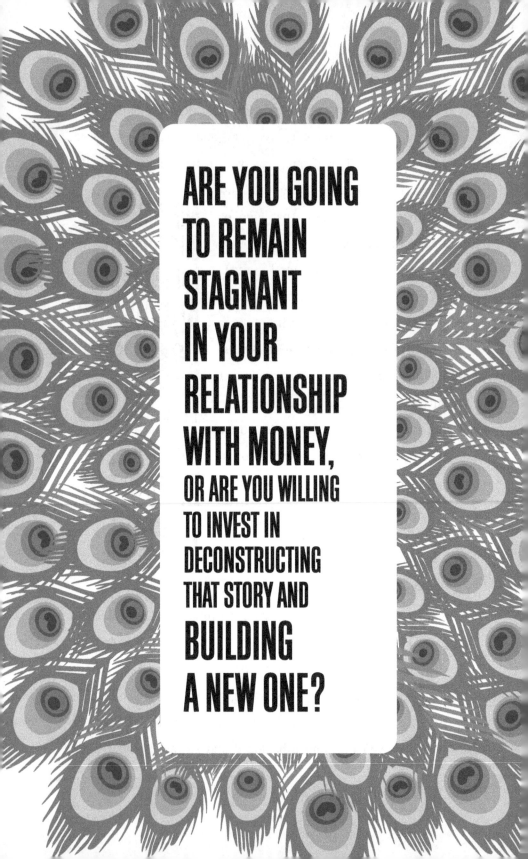

ARE YOU GOING
TO REMAIN
STAGNANT
IN YOUR
RELATIONSHIP
WITH MONEY,
OR ARE YOU WILLING
TO INVEST IN
DECONSTRUCTING
THAT STORY AND
BUILDING
A NEW ONE?

to spending. Consider implementing strategies such as budgeting envelopes, spending caps, or automatic transfers to streamline your finances and stay on track toward your objectives. Regularly revisit and revise your budget as your financial circumstances evolve.

Becoming comfortable with digging into your money story can facilitate freedom from shame, embarrassment, and anxiety. Love yourself enough to trust that until now, you have done the best you could given your money story. And then love yourself enough to figure out a different path if the story needs revising. Don't wait. Spend time dissecting the stories in which you have become invested and rewrite them. Who was that voice shaming you for not knowing how to manage your money? It wasn't you. It was your inner critic. That is a barrier we all share to different degrees. Turn the page.

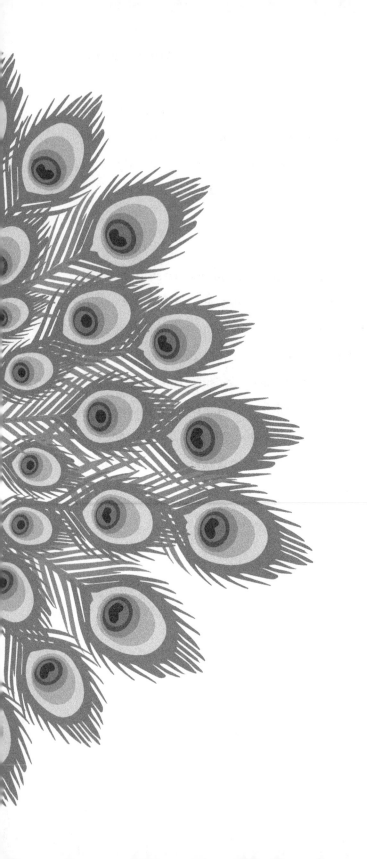

# CHAPTER 7

# THE INNER CRITIC

After more than a decade at ESPN, I needed to face the fact that I wasn't *really* doing what I'd promised myself when Peter passed. When he died on the *SportsCenter* newsroom floor, I vowed never again to wait for the "right time." Yet I harbored a secret desire to report on camera for 10 years before the first live television experience you read about in chapter 4. Peter was only 37 years old at the end of his life, and at the time, my 37th birthday was fast approaching.

I needed to keep my word, but I hadn't told anyone about my desire because my inner critic was working overtime.

That voice in the back of my mind said I wasn't ready. It said other people would judge me for being vain and label me as "attention-seeking." It warned me that I wasn't qualified and would never be able to make the move from producer to reporter. My inner critic told me I would probably be terrible on camera and embarrass myself in front of everyone.

My throat was tight as I stood outside the stadium before my first live report, and I berated myself for trying to go on air. "Why?" I lamented. I had a great job as a producer at ESPN. Why did I put myself in such an uncomfortable position? My then-husband, Matt, tried to calm me down over the phone.

"What is the worst that can happen?" he asked as I wiped away tears.

My exaggerated fear story spilled out, but this wasn't an exercise to find the absurdity in my fear—it was spontaneous Catastrophizing 101: "I could be so bad that I will never get another job in front of the camera and also lose my producing position because the reporters will never take my direction again when they discover how bad I am at their job. My entire television career could go up in flames over this! Then I'll be so unhappy and difficult to live with that I could be a terrible mother, and you will have no choice but to leave me to provide a happier life for our children. Without a job or family, I will probably end up dying penniless and alone."

After a moment of silence, Matt exhaled, "Wow, you went there." Oh yes, I went all the way there.

There is no one we hear more loudly than the voice in our head. It has free reign day and night to jabber away. Our external critics can't hold a candle to the brutality of the things we tell ourselves. Yet no one lies to us more than that voice. Our inner critic is a fraud. It creates all kinds of imaginative disasters. It is a master catastrophizer.

Just as I encourage you to let fear in instead of trying to push it away, do the same with your negative thoughts by shining a light on them to remove their power. It takes too much effort to shove them down. They don't go away; they just go underground and pop up at our most vulnerable moments. Our inner critic attacks when we are uncomfortable, stretched, and in unfamiliar territory.

**THERE IS NO ONE WE HEAR MORE LOUDLY THAN THE VOICE IN OUR HEAD.**

That voice will say you aren't qualified. You will fail. It will urge you to procrastinate with, "Later, when . . ." When I have more time, more money, more credentials. If our critic were a person, we would avoid them like the plague! None of us would want to hang out with someone who erodes our sense of self-worth and makes us feel ashamed, guilty, small, and miserable.

## The Id, Superego, and Ego

Sigmund Freud conducted research in the early 20th century identifying three distinct components of the human psyche: the id, the superego, and the ego. By his definition, the id is driven by instinctual impulses satisfying basic needs. The superego is concerned with being socially acceptable and fitting into norms. The ego tries to find the balance between the two.[5]

According to Freud's findings, as very young infants, we quickly learn how to fit in, how to optimize a sense of love and belonging, and how to gain acceptance and approval from people around us.[6] Losing appreciation and affection as a dependent child is deeply painful and leaves us feeling vulnerable and alone. The superego programs a belief system that influences our impulses and actions while punishing us with feelings of anxiety, inferiority, and guilt for behavior it deems too risky.

Part of our inner critic is undoubtedly the superego trying to protect us from the id's desires. When we don't vet our limiting beliefs and instead accept them as fact, we shut down the id's urge to expand and grow.

In the last chapter, we discussed money as a barrier and how it can be difficult to justify wanting an abundance of it. Maryalice struggled with her inner critic chastising her for pursuing money by whispering, "That's not you." Growing up in a frugal and humble family, Maryalice's desire for money left her feeling ashamed. The goal of creating financial abundance was her id talking. If you allow yourself to desire, your ego will find a realistic way of making it happen. You need to tell your superego that you are worthy and shut down the voice in your head.

The superego wants us to be the same as everyone else, to blend into the shadows and not draw attention for fear that by being unique, we are left out on a ledge without a harness. Our families, cultures, and organizations have a lot of norms and values, standard ways of doing things, and classifications of what is right and wrong. Our communities have an unspoken expectation of how we should behave, and our superego does all it can to shove us into that box.

According to Freud, the ego is the only part of the personality that is conscious.[7] It is what people are aware of when thinking about themselves and what they usually try to project toward others. The ego is the decision-maker and works by reason. The ego's goal is to satisfy the id's demands in safe and socially acceptable ways. It may direct you to compromise or postpone satisfaction to avoid negative societal consequences. Your superego might try to shrink your goals, attempting to keep you safe and within the norm. If a plan of action does not work, the reality-based ego will use

**IF YOU ALLOW YOURSELF TO DESIRE, YOUR EGO WILL FIND A REALISTIC WAY OF MAKING IT HAPPEN.**

reason to find a solution—but only if we can keep the overprotective superego in check.

| Id | Ego | Superego |

The process may look something like this: Your id comes up with this random, crazy, satisfying idea. Your ego looks at that idea and says, "Ok, I see what you are thinking. Let me make a few tweaks to make this a possibility." Then your superego comes in and is the ultimate party pooper, delivering these lines: "I can't do this." "I don't have the qualifications." "People will judge me." "I'm not worthy." "I don't deserve this." "I'm not ready yet." "This is too hard." "I can't change." "I don't have enough _____" (time, money, resources, etc.). "I'm not good at ___."

Our goal is to reduce the superego's chatter to harmless background noise, which will allow us to examine the urge and see if it is the best move to drive us toward a more audacious life. Your superego is the home of imposter syndrome. How do we keep the superego from sabotaging our audacious goals? By first recognizing that those thoughts are not who we are.

## Name Your Inner Critic

In the previous chapters, we have worked through our stories surrounding fear, time, and money. The first step in taming your inner critic is to name it, which is an easy way to separate it from ourselves.

**OUR GOAL IS TO REDUCE THE SUPEREGO'S CHATTER TO HARMLESS BACKGROUND NOISE.**

When writing this chapter, I had a conversation with my 11-year-old daughter, Leyna, asking her about the negative thoughts that creep into her mind regularly. Most of them are related to either school or body image: "I'm stupid," "I'm fat," and "I can't do this" are the three she tells herself most often. We went through the typical questions: Would she talk like that to her friends? Of course she wouldn't! I told her that if it isn't Leyna talking like that, then we need to give that voice a name. She named her critic Jerry.

Many psychology experts suggest that naming our inner critic helps us separate it from our identity. Now, every time my daughter notices those negative thoughts, she assigns them to Jerry. I asked Leyna what she wanted to say to Jerry when she heard him saying she wasn't good enough. The answer was quick: "Shut up, Jerry!"

As you work to keep your critic in check, notice when negative thoughts run through your head. The more you practice, the easier it will become to be aware of the whispers of doubt and inferiority. Give that voice a name. Ideally, not the name of a specific person but rather a fictional character. I wouldn't give a real person free rent in my head—and neither should you—so pick a generic name. Once you experience how unpleasant your not-so-superego is to be around, you might stop taking its advice!

As you assign a personality to the author of those thoughts, you begin to view them as separate from yourself. That is a major accomplishment! Celebrate when you disconnect that negativity from your identity! Most people believe that voice. They think it is based in fact, so they don't question the message. When we truly recognize those are just thoughts and disconnect them from our identity, we can then investigate the message. Are we truly not ready? By whose standards are we not good enough? Who are we afraid will judge us? When we no longer have emotion attached, we have room to be curious about those messages rather than fear them.

## Respond to Your Superego

My response to my superego saboteur is, "That is not helpful." I wanted my response to be as close as possible to what I might say to an outsider offering unconstructive criticism, and I needed it to be void of emotion. My saboteur can say whatever it wants, but its opinion is as worthless to me as an anonymous troll on X (formerly Twitter).

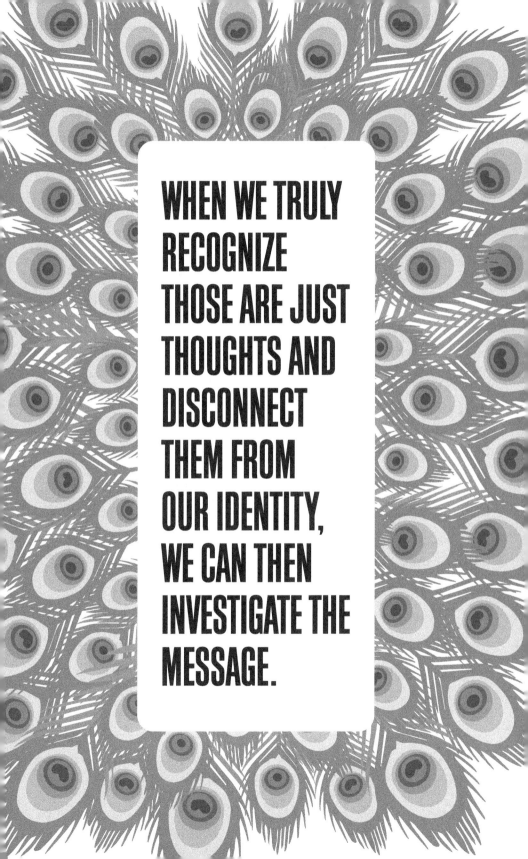

WHEN WE TRULY
RECOGNIZE
THOSE ARE JUST
THOUGHTS AND
DISCONNECT
THEM FROM
OUR IDENTITY,
WE CAN THEN
INVESTIGATE THE
MESSAGE.

Our inner critic is not logical. It is not rational. It is simply a thought. Adults, on average, have 60,000 thoughts a day. According to research, 75 percent of our thoughts are negative, and 95 percent are repetitive.[8] Given those numbers, we all have a massive opportunity to redirect those 45,000 repetitive negative thoughts into positive drivers of our dreams and goals. If we pick apart those thoughts without emotion, is there any grain of information that might be helpful?

Missy West, a speaker who teaches people how to crush their inner critic, started to examine the negativity in her head when she was an elite collegiate basketball player at Duke University. "I created a visual cue when I needed to reset. When I noticed negative thoughts, I would look at the rim to keep me present, then move on to the next." Whether it was playing in the NCAA title game or completing an Ironman race, Missy found herself in a battle with her inner critic. She emphasizes that no one is immune to at least some degree of negative self-talk.

Missy shared that during the relentless exertion of an Ironman, her brain would frequently give way to the superego. "Sometimes, when you are exhausted because you have been on the bike for hours, that voice creeps in. Your inner critic starts planting little seeds of doubt in your ear and drops a healthy dose of fear right on your lap. Fear that you are not going to finish."

Bestselling author Elizabeth Gilbert described her fear and self-doubt in her book, *Big Magic*, as a passenger on a road trip with creativity (id) and her (superego):

> There's plenty of room in this vehicle for all of us, so make yourself at home, but understand this: *Creativity and I are the only ones who will be making any decisions along the way.* I recognize and respect that you are part of this family, and so I will never exclude you from our activities, but still— your suggestions will never be followed. You're allowed to have a seat, and you're allowed to have a voice, but you are not allowed to have a vote. You're not allowed to touch the road maps; you're not allowed to suggest detours; you're not allowed to fiddle with the temperature. Dude, you're not even allowed to touch the radio. But above all else, my dear old familiar friend, you are absolutely forbidden to drive.[9]

By conversing with your inner critic, you begin the process of reframing the experience. Missy suggests a mantra to begin the conversation. While turning her eyes to the rim as a visual cue in a basketball game helped her reset, Missy battled significant anxiety when she first began working as a keynote speaker. To disarm the negative thoughts when she took to the stage, Missy trained herself to look at the spot in the back of the room where the wall met the ceiling. When she felt her critic creeping in, she would focus on that spot and silently repeat, "Where the wall meets the ceiling is a wonderful feeling."

"When I no longer had a rim as my visual reset, I needed something that was going to be present in every situation. I can always find the spot where a wall meets the ceiling. Anytime I get nervous,

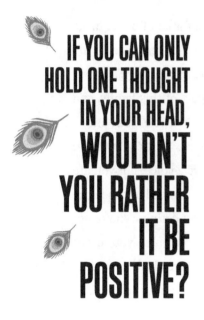

**IF YOU CAN ONLY HOLD ONE THOUGHT IN YOUR HEAD, WOULDN'T YOU RATHER IT BE POSITIVE?**

I repeat my mantra, and that softens my mind and eases my anxiety. You cannot hold a positive and a negative thought in your head at the same time."

A mantra is metaphorically sweeping the critic's chatter out of your head to make room for your audacious mindset. It can snap you out of going down an unhelpful rabbit hole. Remember that the key to an audacious mindset is optimism. Optimism is the belief that somehow everything will work out. If you can only hold one thought in your head, wouldn't you rather it be positive?

Once we start to pay attention to our self-talk, we may be surprised by its occasional cruelty. By seeing our thoughts as outside of ourselves, we separate the superego's negativity from the ego's reality. We are not those negative thoughts—they are just thoughts. The superego is full of limiting beliefs delivered with a disapproving tone and negative chatter. Those limiting beliefs and negative thoughts are "Jerry," emanating from a source other than our true selves.

It isn't that our superego doesn't have a place in our life. It certainly does. It is our moral compass, and it adds value in many ways. For example, if you feel the urge to take home office supplies from work, it is your superego that counteracts that urge by reminding you stealing is wrong. The superego can promote positive affirmations and raise our self-esteem when we make a morally or ethically sound decision. I'm not suggesting you shut your superego down altogether (frankly, that would be impossible); I'm asking you to notice what it is telling you and remove emotional attachment to it so you can examine its message for validity.

The superego is both a saboteur and a safety valve. It is our job to determine if the risk is reckless or worth it.

## Mantras and Visual Cues

Missy stresses that creating a mantra and a visual cue is helpful in all areas of life. "I recently spoke with a group of oncologists. I asked them to picture being in a difficult surgery when a complication arises. Perhaps it is something they have never seen before. Every operating room has a clock, so I suggested they lift their head, gaze briefly at the clock, and fill their mind with messages of competence." For Missy, her message of competence meant internalizing thoughts such as, *I have trained years for this, and although I have never seen this problem before, I have worked through other difficult situations. I am the most capable person to handle this challenge. I am going to figure this out and get better today. My intentions are good.*

When anxiety or doubt creeps in, my mantra is, "I am supported by my feet on the ground." It is a fact that leaves no room for dispute. If my head is entertaining fantasies not based in reality, I want an indisputable truth. Rather than a visual cue, I like a physical reset. I wiggle my toes inside my shoes while thinking *I am supported by my feet on the ground.* No one can see it, but I can feel it. It is a reminder that no matter the situation, I am supported.

Sometimes, our inner critic repeats things that others have said to us. It plants the thought: *Were they right about me?* This is especially true when the message comes from someone whose opinion we value.

When I was 11, my father called me cocky. It was a passing comment by a man who had always been my biggest cheerleader. I have no idea why it stuck with me the way it did, but I allowed it to play a part in stunting my transition from being behind the scenes to in front of the camera. The thought that I might be cocky played on a loop in my head for decades. As I was writing this chapter, I looked up the definition of cocky: *Someone who is cocky is so confident and sure of their abilities that they annoy other people.*[10]

Wait a minute! Cocky means my confidence annoys other people? WHAT?! That completely changes the meaning and the way I feel about it. "So confident and sure of their abilities." Yes, that's me—because I limit my negative self-talk. The second part of the definition, "that they annoy other people"—I don't care. Seriously, I legitimately don't care if my confidence annoys other people. *That*

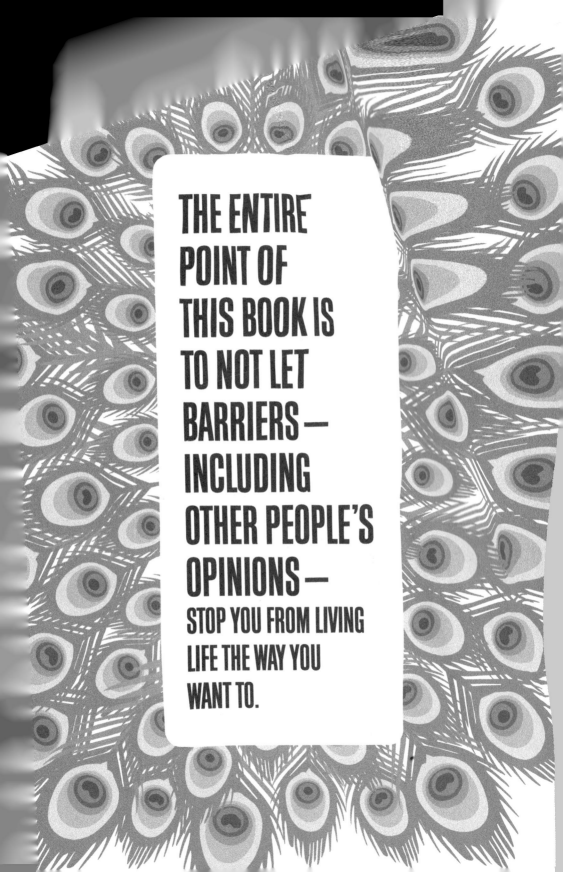

THE ENTIRE
POINT OF
THIS BOOK IS
TO NOT LET
BARRIERS—
INCLUDING
OTHER PEOPLE'S
OPINIONS—
STOP YOU FROM LIVING
LIFE THE WAY YOU
WANT TO.

*is their problem.* The point of this book is to not let *but* including other perceptions—stop you from living life the way you want to.

For four decades I carried a different definition of cocky in my head. I thought that cocky meant being overconfident with a diminished ability, as in a person thinking they are great at something when their ability is solidly in the norm. With that new definition, being called cocky is a freaking compliment. Who doesn't want to be confident and sure of their abilities?

## Manage Your Inner Critic

Just like Elizabeth Gilbert's road trip with fear and creativity, your inner critic will be along for the ride on your audacious journey, whether you like it or not. It's not about getting rid of your inner critic but managing it. Try the steps below for learning to manage the voice inside your head.

Be **Aware:** The first step is becoming aware of what your inner critic says. When and in which situations does it arise? Notice what your inner critic is saying in those moments. Pause and reflect on the message the critic is sending. Be curious about it, but don't let it take control of your actions. Keep a log of your negative or dysfunctional thoughts for a week, noting how many there are and the variety. Use the following questions to help:

When did the thought occur?

What was the context (what was happening at the time and prior to the thought)?

On a scale of 1 to 10, how much did you believe the thought?

What did you feel?

How was the thought distorted?

What is a different potential outcome?

**Label It:** Whether you want to call it a villain, joker, thief, or Jerry, your inner critic is not you. Name the voice inside your head and recognize the thoughts it feeds you as separate from yourself.

**Go for It:** You only learn by doing. And while your inner critic wants to keep you safe and socially acceptable, it can also hold you back from taking the worth it risks necessary to live audaciously.

After working through the stories attached to our barriers—fear, time, money, and the inner critic—there is only one thing left to do. It is time to come up with a plan. I don't espouse throwing caution to the wind and metaphorically jumping out of the plane and hoping for the best. You need to pack your parachute. That begins by building a support system of people and resources to keep you focused on the goal and leave everything that doesn't align with that goal out of the equation. How to do that? Turn the page.

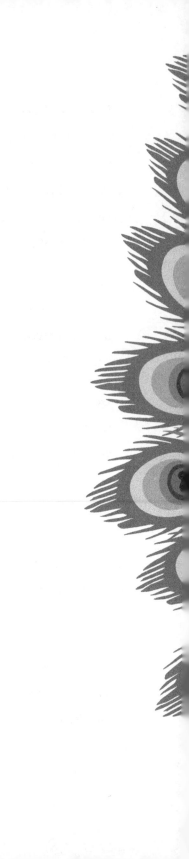

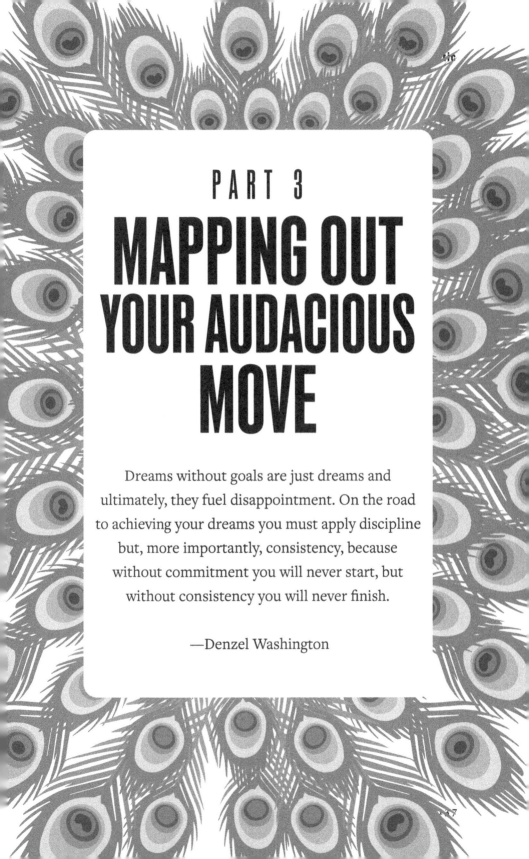

# PART 3
# MAPPING OUT YOUR AUDACIOUS MOVE

Dreams without goals are just dreams and ultimately, they fuel disappointment. On the road to achieving your dreams you must apply discipline but, more importantly, consistency, because without commitment you will never start, but without consistency you will never finish.

—Denzel Washington

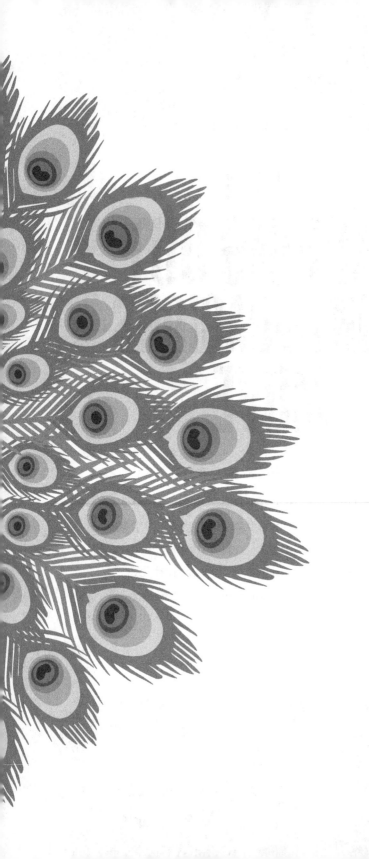

# CHAPTER 8

# HOW TO PACK YOUR PARACHUTE

In the fall of 2003, I worked 12 games as a sideline reporter on the weekends while producing during the week; the other nine months of the year, I produced full time. In 2004, I did a dozen more games on air. I continued to produce *SportsCenter* news coverage during the week. I was stiff and uncomfortable in front of the camera, and my improvement was slow.

One of my supervisors, whom I trusted, bluntly told me, "You are never going to be good on air if you continue producing." He explained the only way to improve was by consistently reporting. I wouldn't be on camera enough to see real gains if I continued along my current path. It was time, he said, to make a decision. Was I going to go all in on reporting, or did I want to continue as a producer? Being on camera was a coveted position, but I wasn't confident that I could garner enough assignments to make it a career. Producing was safer since I had already established success.

I backtracked and chose to produce, then took leave to give birth to my first child—I needed a secure job, and producing provided that security. Two and a half months after my son was born, I returned to producing. My first assignment was coverage of a sensitive story with veteran reporter Shelley Smith. Shelley is a nine-time Emmy Award winner and a good friend. We worked together for many years, and I admired her versatility. She was a single mother who, a decade earlier, had brought her daughter, Dylann, on assignment with us when she was just six years old. "Bring the baby," Shelley urged me when we were assigned together.

A *SportsCenter* breaking news assignment like this meant we needed to leave almost immediately. There wasn't time to arrange childcare. My husband was an accountant, and it was tax season, so he couldn't take care of a 10-week-old indefinitely. I was breast-feeding anyway, so it made sense for me to bring Lukas.

Shelley was incredibly patient as the baby screamed on the flight and in the car. The assignment didn't have a specific end date. We were covering a story about a college football player accused of murder, and there were several key people we needed to find and interview. We flew from Colorado to Phoenix before our leads took us to Los Angeles. Lukas's crying was keeping me up all night and affecting the quality of my work as we bounced from city to city.

Finally, I broke. I called my boss and cried, "I can't do this." It was the same supervisor who had told me a year earlier that I needed consistent on-air repetitions if I wanted to improve. I admitted I needed to leave the unpredictable schedule of a field producer and find a position with a schedule my husband and I could plan around.

Working on games meant having a schedule months in advance rather than the immediacy of *SportsCenter* news coverage as a producer. If I were to become a full-time live event reporter, we could plan childcare well in advance of my assignments.

It made sense for me to go all in on becoming a reporter. I needed to plan how I was going to finally make the audacious move on camera full time. As I prepared to jump, it was time to pack my parachute.

## What's in Your Parachute?

What do I mean by a parachute? Taking a bold risk is undoubtedly a leap of faith. Before anyone takes a scary jump—out of a plane, for example—we need to have a "parachute of plans" to mitigate the risk. By my definition, a parachute is *not* a rip cord so you can bail and let your fears, obstacles, and doubts derail your goals. Instead, packing your parachute means compiling all the things you need to set yourself up for a safe and softer landing as you embark on a new journey.

At this point, you have explored what has been stopping you from leaping from your current situation to the one you want to have. As you considered your barriers while working through chapters 4 through 7, your personal packing plan was laid before you. Reflect upon what you learned. Lean into whatever is most uncomfortable and consider what you would need in terms of support to feel more confident related to that obstacle. Take your time to pick through each barrier thoroughly as you lay out your plan.

### Fear

What fears did you identify in chapter 4? They are different for all of us. My fears about going on camera centered upon embarrassment and judgment. I knew I wasn't good. I hated the sound of my voice and my delivery. It was embarrassing to be bad at a job in front of my colleagues who were consummate pros. As a producer, I was even more aware than many other newbies on air of my awkwardness and faults. I knew what I needed to do to become more fluid in my presentation, but knowing what to do and executing it were

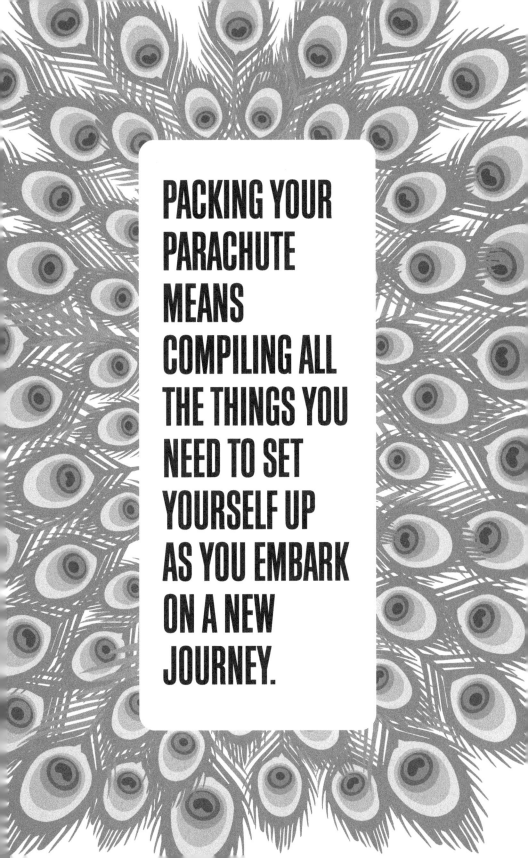

PACKING YOUR PARACHUTE MEANS COMPILING ALL THE THINGS YOU NEED TO SET YOURSELF UP AS YOU EMBARK ON A NEW JOURNEY.

very different. I suspected viewers, and maybe even some friends and colleagues, would judge my performance unkindly.

To pack your parachute and allay your fears, write down what you're afraid of. Catastrophize them. Assess how likely it is that you will reach that end. Will you really die destitute and alone, or will the outcome, even in a poor situation, fall short of complete ruin? Then, consider your ability to survive the potential negative consequences of your fear. I was indeed an awkward reporter when I began on camera, but I survived. I was afraid I would be embarrassed, and I certainly was, but I survived that too and worked to get better. I had fears that some of my friends and colleagues would judge my performance, and they did. I still survived and eventually thrived.

### Time

Chapter 5 was all about time and the urgency fallacy. Clearly, my producing position had been urgent. After receiving a *SportsCenter* assignment, I'd usually head to the airport in a day or two. With a newborn, I found it nearly impossible to produce at a high level while pursuing what was professionally important—improving my on-camera presence. When I decided producing was no longer an option, I needed to learn how to navigate the urgency of raising a child with the important (to me) goal of reporting on camera. My biggest challenge with time while producing was the lack of notice as to when and for how long I would need childcare. With a schedule of games months in advance for reporting, I could budget my time in line with my goals.

It is important that you clearly define what is important to you and allocate time accordingly. That may mean not spending all of your time pursuing your audacious goal at the expense of urgency. You will still need to do your current job, pay your bills, and spend time with your family. So, create a time budget that sets aside the specific time you plan to spend on your next move. Put it in your calendar and stick to it, even if that means finding four 15-minute slots per day.

## *Money*

What did you discover as you examined your money story? There needs to be a balance between earning, spending, and saving. I cringe when I hear someone put all their savings into their latest idea. Audacious living is not about living on the edge. Recognize where your strengths are in your relationship with money. Can you trade money to have more time or energy to pursue your goal, as I did when I hired an assistant? Should you tighten up spending in other areas to reallocate that money toward your goals?

When it came time for me to consider money as a potential barrier, I was very lucky to have not only had a frugal upbringing, but my ex-husband was also a saver. Our money story as a couple was an awareness of how to live within our means. One of the gifts of our marriage was that we never fought about money. Matt was supportive of my move to reporting. After all, he didn't want me to leave him with a baby on zero notice! We ran the numbers and knew it wouldn't be comfortable, but we were confident that slight adjustments in our spending would allow us room for this change.

Write down how much money you spend pursuing your goal and look for balance. If you are putting a lot of money in and not getting much in return, it is time to recalibrate.

## Inner Critic

What kind of things does your inner critic say as you prepare to take the audacious leap? Practice recognizing that those messages are not facts but rather unrealized fears. Separate them from yourself. Thank them and move on. I say "thank them" because when you acknowledge them, you aren't trying to push those thoughts down but rather letting them surface and choosing not to follow that path. Make a decision whether or not to follow your critic! Most often, your critic spews random thoughts that are not helpful as you make your way toward a more satisfying life.

When I transitioned to being on camera, I had not yet separated my inner critic from my own voice, but my mindset as a former collegiate athlete was a great help. In athletics, no one is "good" when they start playing a new sport. It takes many mistakes, losses, and failures to become proficient. Just as I had worked consistently as a volleyball player to be a little bit better each time I took to the court, I knew I would have to have the same patience on air. I quieted my inner critic as often as possible and focused on incremental steps to improve.

In packing your parachute, deliberately examine, address, and create workable plans for each of your obstacles. Create budgets for both time and money. How it is spent, saved, and what you can bank for the eras when it gets extra challenging. Do the work digging into your fears and catastrophizing your situation. My exaggerated fear story ended with me dying destitute and alone. We worked on that story for exactly this moment. When you are ready to jump, recognize that no matter the outcome, it is highly unlikely to end with your complete demise. Acknowledge and name your inner critic. Don't try to suppress it when it arises, but be aware that it is just your superego defense mechanism attempting to keep you safe. I thank that voice and follow it up with, "Those are just thoughts that are not helpful right now."

## IN PACKING YOUR PARACHUTE, DELIBERATELY EXAMINE, ADDRESS, AND CREATE WORKABLE PLANS FOR EACH OF YOUR OBSTACLES.

## Build Your Front Row

No one does it alone. Who are the people who want to see you succeed without jealousy? I call those people my *front row*. Your front row should ideally consist of individuals who genuinely want to see you thrive, including family members, close friends, mentors, and peers who share your aspirations or have experience in the areas you're pursuing. They are the people who not only cheer you on but also hold you accountable to your goals.

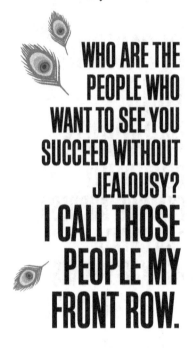

**WHO ARE THE PEOPLE WHO WANT TO SEE YOU SUCCEED WITHOUT JEALOUSY? I CALL THOSE PEOPLE MY FRONT ROW.**

I work out several times a week with two friends. Every Monday, Wednesday, and Friday (barring travel), Holly, Nicole, and I meet to work out. We have an ongoing text chain with the typical short comments, memes, and chatter peppered with "Don't forget to sign up for class" and "Are you both coming to work out tomorrow morning?" Those two friends are in my fitness front row, meaning if I don't show up, they aren't letting it slide. The thing that is important to me (fitness in this case) is also very important to them. We hold each other accountable.

We can have multiple front rows that support us in different areas of our lives.

My personal front row is made up of the friends I confided in first about my divorce. I felt like a failure and feared people were going to judge me. I had a huge amount of shame that I couldn't fix the marriage, and it took me almost a year after my marriage ended to tell anyone that Matt and I had split. I flew to New York and cried my eyes out with three friends I've known since my teens. Gradually, I told my four brothers one by one, each time fearful of the reaction. But they all supported me, asking, "What do you need?" They listened quietly on the phone while I sobbed.

Matt, my ex-husband, is in my parenting front row. We made a pact to skip the drama and present a united front to the kids. Without the pressure of the marriage, we ended up becoming better friends after we split.

Building your front row is about finding the people willing to talk you off the ledge of uncertainty and imposter syndrome, even when you don't want to hear it. You can be comfortable failing in front of that squad. You have witnessed their failures and triumphs too.

Some people in your professional front row may be colleagues or people already in the field you are pursuing. I had tremendous support from my reporter colleagues when I wanted to make the move from being behind the camera to on air. They worked with me as I recorded myself to create video footage to use in job applications. They shared the tips that they had learned along the path in their careers.

When writing this book, I reached out to a few authors I admired but did not know personally. They were very supportive: I could call and ask about publishing companies or keynote speaker protocols.

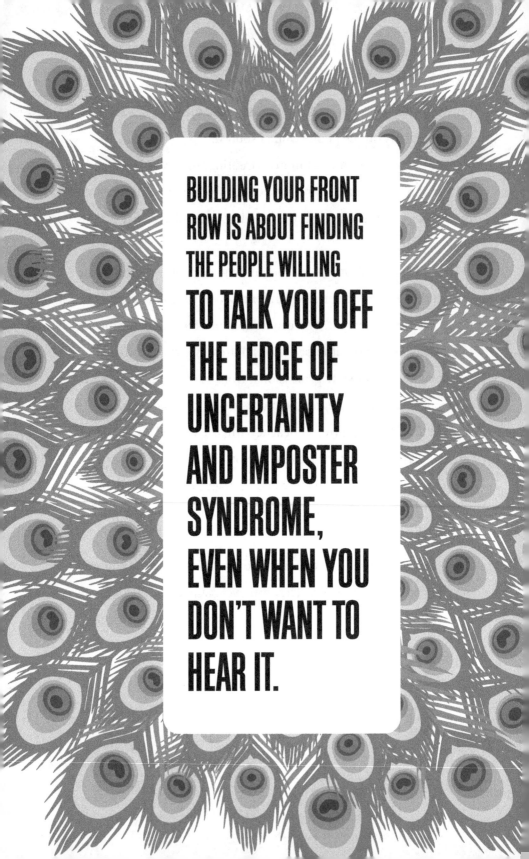

BUILDING YOUR FRONT ROW IS ABOUT FINDING THE PEOPLE WILLING **TO TALK YOU OFF THE LEDGE OF UNCERTAINTY AND IMPOSTER SYNDROME, EVEN WHEN YOU DON'T WANT TO HEAR IT.**

## Choose Your Front Row Wisely

However, as important as building that front row is, it's equally crucial to recognize who should *not* be in your support circle. A woman once asked after a keynote, "Is it possible to have a back row?" I laughed, but she brought up a good point. There are those who you not only shouldn't let in your front row but who shouldn't even be allowed in the room.

**IT'S EQUALLY CRUCIAL TO RECOGNIZE WHO SHOULD NOT BE IN YOUR SUPPORT CIRCLE.**

Negative influences, skeptics, or individuals who consistently undermine your goals and aspirations can hinder your progress and drain your motivation. It's essential to prioritize your well-being and surround yourself with positivity and encouragement.

Be careful of the well-meaning fear-monger. Potential saboteurs have their own reasons for trying to talk you out of changing things up, including:

- They don't want you to be hurt or disappointed.
- They have anxiety about making changes in their own life.
- They're jealous of your chutzpah and afraid that your success will diminish their accomplishments by comparison.
- It's comfortable for you to stay the same because they fear your relationship with them will change otherwise.
- They project their fear of failure onto you.

You may love your mother, but it doesn't mean she belongs in your front row. Parents' own experiences with risk and adversity can shape their attitudes about risk-taking in their children. If parents have experienced failure, disappointment, or hardship in a particular area, they may be more inclined to shield their children from similar experiences out of a desire to spare them pain or disappointment.

Parents also may have specific ideas or expectations about what constitutes success for their children, and they may believe that avoiding risks will increase their children's chances of accomplishment. This mindset can lead parents to prioritize safety and stability over exploration and risk-taking.

When faced with well-intentioned discouragement from individuals in your circle, approach the situation with empathy and understanding, but also assertiveness. Communicate your feelings and explain how their pessimistic words or actions impact you. Encourage open dialogue and express your need for positivity and reassurance as you pursue your goals. Ultimately, surrounding yourself with a supportive network of individuals who uplift and empower you can fuel your confidence, resilience, and determination as you navigate life's audacious moves.

It can be heartbreaking to discover that someone you thought was in your corner is happiest when your light doesn't shine bright. Sometimes people want to keep us small to avoid examining their own hesitancy to grow. If you start to notice jealousy or competition creeping into their comments, take note and create distance. If someone is indirectly or actively undermining you, not only are they not in your front row, but they shouldn't have a seat at all.

That doesn't mean you should only surround yourself with people who praise every move you make. A true supporter will tell you when they see something that might be taking you off track. Evaluate whose opinions you can trust to question you from a place of support. You don't want a room full of yes-men when taking bold risks. You want friends who have your very best interests at heart without competition.

When you look at your current life, who is in your front row? The core people who show up for you no matter the situation. They hold you accountable and help you move forward. And they are just as supportive of your aspirations when you aren't in the room as they are standing by your side, cheering you on and asking the critical questions.

Beware of getting caught in the cycle of packing and repacking your parachute indefinitely, wanting it to be perfect. It will never be perfect, and you will never have all the answers, but you are ready. You have everything you need. You have done the work examining your barriers. You have a plan for each obstacle. It's not a perfect plan—but it will do. None of this is set in stone. You have identified your front row. The "right time" is not coming, so don't wait for it. Waiting doesn't work. This is the right time. Right now. The next step is to take the leap. Let's go. Turn the page.

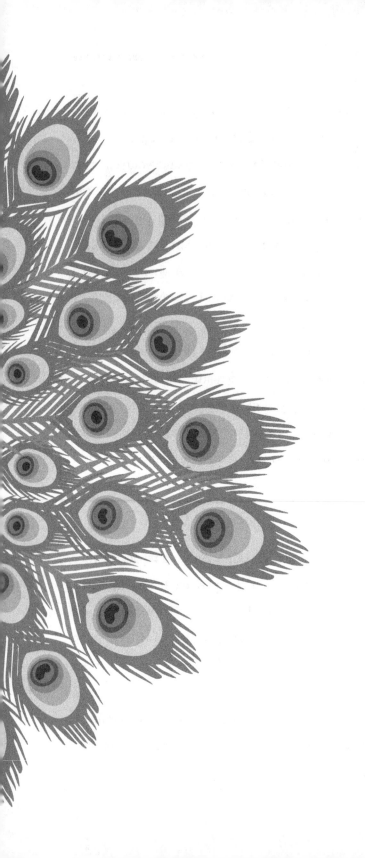

CHAPTER

9

# JUMP!

I had just finished delivering my Cultivating Audacity keynote to a group of educators at a women in leadership conference in New Hampshire when an attendee approached me in the hallway. She explained she had been a teacher for 28 years but had always wanted to be an assistant principal. She felt she could have a bigger impact on more students in that role but was nervous about the application process. The assistant principal position at her school was opening, and she asked me to help her brainstorm about how to approach applying for the job. As we discussed how she could get there, she mentioned that her principal was at the conference.

"Wait, what?" I asked, "He is here? Did he just hear my keynote?" He had indeed been in the audience. I asked what conversations she'd had with him about wanting to take on the new role. The answer was none: She hadn't mustered the courage to bring it up yet. She had thought about it for years, knew the qualifications, and had spent an inordinate amount of time working up the nerve to approach him.

I smiled, and she groaned, "You are going to say I should do this right now, aren't you?" Yep. I encouraged

**IT IS TIME FOR YOU TO DO YOUR THING.**

her to walk up to the principal, tell him her goal, and ask if they could set up a meeting to talk about it. She told me she had a good relationship with him and felt he was always supportive. The talk was fresh in his mind, so we decided she would say, "I have been teaching for decades and am ready to take on a bigger task. I am going to apply for the assistant principal job. *Will you be in my front row?*"

I hunted her down three times at that conference, asking if she had done it yet. Each time, she said, "Not yet, but I will," but time was ticking down. I didn't want the conference to end before she asked him.

Finally, I said, "I am going to stand over here and watch you approach him. I'm not leaving until you do."

Not giving her a choice, I watched from a distance as she started the conversation with him. His response was simple, "Of course. All you have to do is ask."

Six weeks later, I received this message from her.

"Hi Anne Marie. This is Brenda. We met at the symposium in New Hampshire in late March. Your advice to find my front-row people and be audacious has led to hard work, a few interviews, and a new position as an assistant principal at my current school. I start July 1st. I am nervous and thrilled and can't wait for this next adventure in my career. I am forever grateful."

That message made my day. Brenda did "the thing," and it is time for you to do your thing too.

## Hope Is Not a Plan

It's not a popular position, but I'm not a big fan of hope. People always argue when I say that: "But hope is a virtue!" they cry. "Hope is the most important thing in life," they stress, "without it, there is no purpose."

At the beginning of this book, we identified optimism as the center of an audacious mindset. Optimism is the belief that things will work out. Not the *hope* that they will work out but the *belief* that if you do the work, everything will be ok. Belief implies certainty and conviction, but it also requires action. Hope can be a weak word. It feels passive—as if we are observers of our lives and not drivers.

I have always been annoyed by the question, "What is plan B?" Like "Plan A is to write a book, but if that doesn't work out, then plan B is to . . ." It is to what? *Not* write a book?

Hope is not a plan. If you want to hope for plan A but have plan B in your back pocket, then you may as well skip plan A altogether and just go straight to plan B. Plan B is always easier. But audacity isn't about easy. It is about growth. And growth is uncomfortable.

## Plan Your Audacious Move

As you take the first tentative steps toward creating a life you are excited to wake up to, remember that you don't have to do it all today. In fact, you can't do it all today. What you *can* do today, though, is take a step. At the beginning of this book, we talked about audacious behavior as an action. Who are the people and what are the systems you need in place to have the freedom to make the move? Below are four steps you can take *today* to start the ball rolling.

### Step 1: Make It Public

The first step in day one of your audacious path is to make it public. Just like Brenda did in the example above, you need to be brave enough to speak what you want into existence. She wanted to be an assistant principal, and then she told her colleague the move she wanted to make. She asked him clearly and specifically if he would be in her front row.

I was speaking at a women's conference in Vermont when, at the Q&A following my keynote, someone raised their hand and asked, "What's next for you?" I replied, "I'm going to write a book about audacity." Then I paused and added, "Damn. I said it aloud. Now I *have* to write the book!" Until then, I had never told anyone my plan. This book went to press less than one year later.

It can be scary to make our plans public because people will know if we fail or give up. That is where your front row comes in.

Call your front row, collectively or individually, and announce what you are going to do. Tell them you are finally going to do "the thing"—that thing they've heard you talking about for years. Their reaction to the news is an audition for your front row. Some friends will be your biggest cheerleaders: "YES, dude, you have been talking about this forever. Let's go!" Other friends will express hesitation or doubt. It doesn't mean they are automatically out of your front row. It means you need to have a brief discussion about their concerns. They may add value by bringing up an idea you had not yet considered. You don't have to explain yourself and don't need to 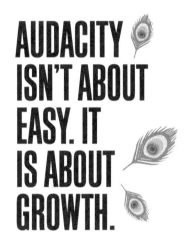 justify your plan. Simply address their concerns and move on. Going forward, you can assess whether they truly belong in your front row. Keep in mind that they are witnessing your audacity from their own prism of experiences, so they may hesitate or even tell you not to do it because they are afraid of the uncertainty. It is understandable that their first instinct may be to protect you from whatever has stood in their way.

Time will tell who deserves a seat on your support team. Announce your plan as a matter of fact: not the projected outcome, but the actual audacious action you are going to take. If you say, "I am going to write a bestselling book," that isn't within your control. You don't have the power to make people buy your book. But if you say to your front row, "I am going to write a book," that is completely within your ability.

Explain to your front row their role in your life. It is an honor to be chosen. When you share that you are going to do something challenging and need their support, many will jump at the chance to be part of the process. Find the friends and colleagues who match your enthusiasm. If they are negative, they aren't qualified. Choose carefully and slowly.

Be specific about what you need from your front row. As I began writing this book, I needed to spend two days mapping it out without the distraction of family. My friend Holly, who has squarely been in my front row from day one, offered me her rental apartment free of charge to work without interruption. There, I could begin the process of laying out chapters and devising a writing plan.

Your front row (if you build it right) consists of people who want you to make this move, and they will naturally prod you if it appears you are slowing down or have lost your focus.

### Step 2: Create an Action Plan

Step two is to set a tangible action plan with a start date. When and how are you going to begin the process of creating the life you want?

"I'm leaving Tuesday" (your job, your relationship, for a trip, etc.): What's the most important part of this? Tuesday! Why is this time different from any of the other times you were going to do this? This time is different because you have publicly declared a starting point.

Whatever you need to do to take that initial leap needs to have a date attached. When will you do it? Not in the spring, not this evening, but Tuesday. Let your front row know your start date so you can receive those texts, "Hey, it is Tuesday. How did it go today?" Accountability is powerful.

Just as you build a foundation before building a house, you need a clear plan for moving from point A to point B to build your dream. Rather than random markers, like, "I will finish writing by May," set a schedule that marks progress. "I will have a rough draft of chapters one and two by February 5."

And then create a task list for reaching that first progress report. "I will leave my phone in the other room and write from 9 to 10 a.m. every weekday and 8 to 10 a.m. every weekend." Be flexible but firm. When writing for one hour a day didn't work for me, I had to use mini sessions that added up to an hour each day. Be flexible on how to reach that first marker, but be firm in that you have no questions about reaching it.

### Step 3: Get Comfortable with Your Obstacles

The third step is to put your most powerful obstacle in your daily eyeline. Remember in chapter 6 when Maryalice Goldsmith had to change her money story? Instead of burying her head in the sand, she worked looking at her bank balance into her morning routine. Money was her greatest obstacle, so she made extra effort to get comfortable with it.

If time is your biggest barrier, set an alarm to carve out one hour each day to work toward your goal. The alarms can be for one hour straight through or 15- or 20-minute intervals. Keep a log of how much time you devote to what is important to you each day. Are you meeting your set goals? If not, does your goal or your plan need adjustment? If you can't reach an hour every day, you need to reallocate your time. For example, maybe three hours every weekend day is a better plan so you can spend less time during the week. You must come face-to-face on a daily basis with what has stopped you up until this point. If you are imprecise about spending your time and logging it, you will never get anywhere. Urgent will always take over.

Whatever obstacles you discovered during chapters 4 through 7 should be part of your daily practice. A little notebook where you tick off the times your inner critic tries to waylay your progress. Maybe you allow yourself to think about your fears as you brush your teeth in the morning but visualize washing them down the drain and focus on your next steps the rest of day.

Make space for your obstacle(s) because, by attempting to shove it down, you will find it popping up when you are most vulnerable. This is what I mean by saying, "Make friends with fear." Acknowledge that this is a challenging area for you and make it part of your daily practice to welcome it in, address it, and then put it aside. It will help assuage the discomfort and prevent it from dominating your day.

### Step 4: Share Your Progress

Create check-ins with your front row. Sharing your progress can be a powerful motivator. Calendar consistent check-in calls with someone who will hold you accountable. In writing this book, I had several methods of sharing my progress. I did a video call with my editor every few weeks, turning in two chapters each time. I had coffee with a friend every two

WHATEVER OBSTACLES YOU DISCOVERED SHOULD BE A PART OF YOUR DAILY PRACTICE.

weeks, where we'd spend an hour talking about my progress and then an hour evaluating her progress. I wrote notes on my wall calendar celebrating what I accomplished each month.

Your check-ins can be on your phone or written on Post-it notes and stuck to your wall. It can be a brief Zoom meeting with a colleague in your desired space, or you can set up coffee with a friend. But I don't recommend giving a progress report while doing something else like walking. You need to focus and ask follow-up questions, write notes, or explore new paths. Check-ins require a high level of concentration. Remember: This is important, not urgent, so have a thoughtful approach.

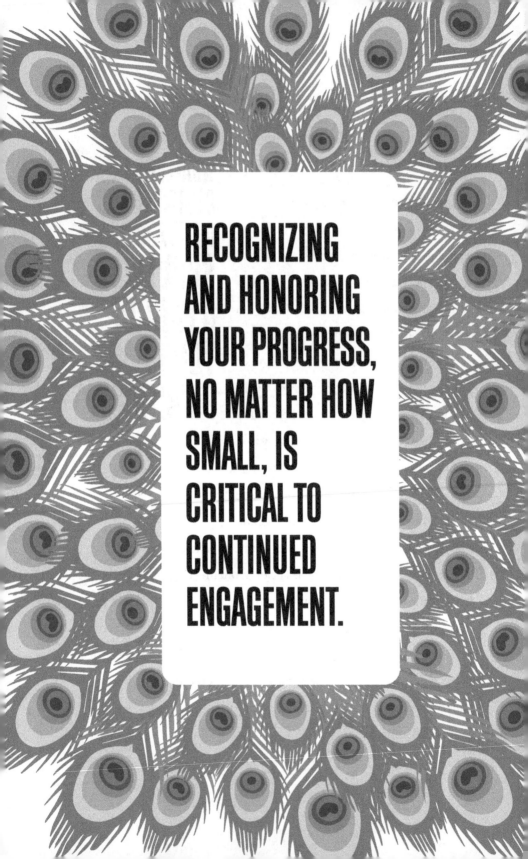

RECOGNIZING AND HONORING YOUR PROGRESS, NO MATTER HOW SMALL, IS CRITICAL TO CONTINUED ENGAGEMENT.

Celebrations should also be a regular part of your routine. When you hit a new milestone, treat yourself to a nice dinner, a round of golf, or a massage. Anything to acknowledge and track your progress so it is broken up into segments rather than just one long odyssey with a destination in mind for the far-out future. The journey will be challenging, but it should also be enjoyable. Recognizing and honoring your progress, no matter how small, is critical to continued engagement.

## When Is the Right Time? (Hint: Now!)

Timing is everything . . . and nothing. You can wait a lifetime for the perfect moment, and it will never arrive. Hearing someone say, "I will do it when . . ." is a sure sign it is never going to happen. Life can slip through your fingers while you search for the right time that never arrives.

Waiting doesn't work. Paralysis from over-analyzing only delays progress.

You are reading this book *now*. You came here to check if it is the right time to make this move. This is your signal. Your confirmation. Yes, now is the right time.

**WAITING DOESN'T WORK.**

I worked at ESPN for a decade before sharing my aspirations of being on air. I let the fear of embarrassment and failure keep me stuck. It was only because of the promise to myself when Peter passed that I could delay no longer.

Peter's death has been a thread throughout my life. When I turned 37 years old, I was reminded his life was only 37 years long. I asked, "What am I going to do with my bonus time?" When I was 37, I had my first child and left producing behind to go full time on air. Since 37, I have created a family, traveled to every continent minus Antarctica, worked for over 10 broadcast networks, become a keynote speaker, written a book, and pushed myself to feel a little uncomfortable every day. It is time Peter didn't have, and I never want to take this time for granted.

You wouldn't be reading this if it wasn't the right time. Here is your signal in print. Don't stay the same. Grow.

You are holding this book in your hands right now. HELLO?! This serves as your unmistakable signal to embark on your audacious journey. You are here, reading these words, because you've already taken a step toward change. The universe is nudging you, telling you the time has come to rise, to shed the armor of hesitation, and to embrace audacity.

If you find yourself on the ledge, ready to leap but hesitating, do the thing that scares you the most first. The big scary thing in the closet that you want to work up to—do that first! Have the experience of failing and surviving first. When you learned how to ride a bike, you fell, it hurt, you got up and tried again and fell again . . . until you didn't. Practice failing. Seek it out.

The more you fail, the easier it is to take another risk. Sometimes, success can paralyze us because we don't want to mess it up, or we wonder if the luck will remain. We temper ourselves with, "I better quit while I am ahead." Failure generates data that allows us to reevaluate our direction.

Jump! You are on your way, but audacious living knows no destination. Turn the page.

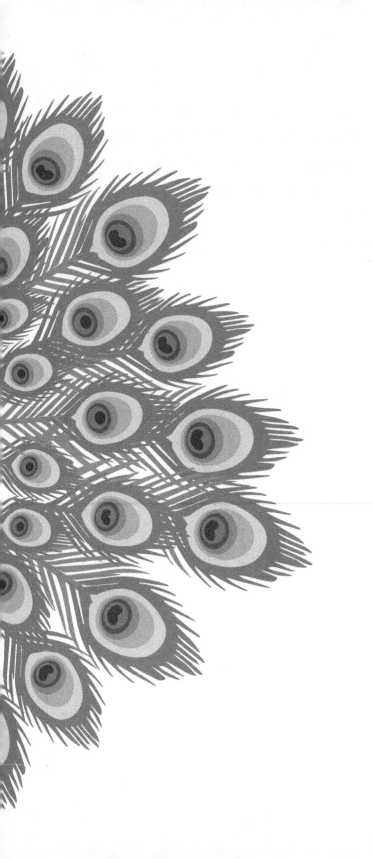

# THE REEVALUATION LOOP

The difference between an audacious move and an audacious life lies in mindful reevaluation. After taking that first terrifying step into reporting, I consistently sought out and got sideline assignments. I was primarily a college football reporter, though I did pick up one-off

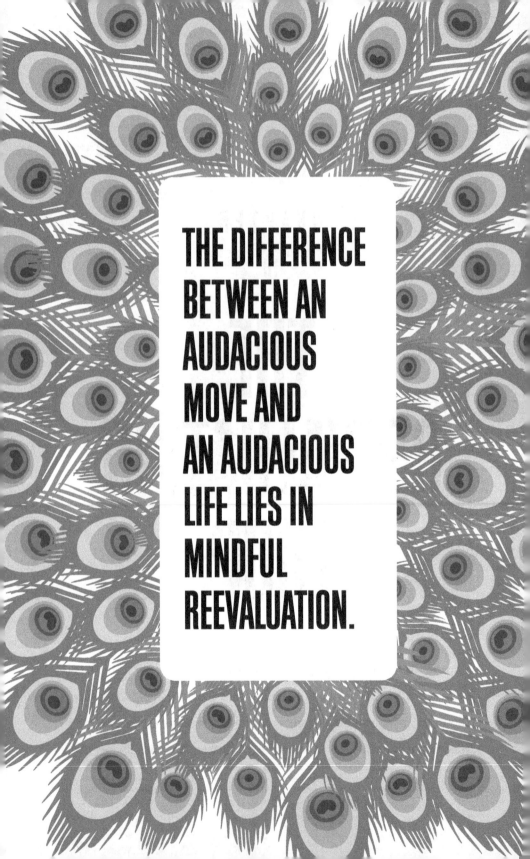

THE DIFFERENCE BETWEEN AN AUDACIOUS MOVE AND AN AUDACIOUS LIFE LIES IN MINDFUL REEVALUATION.

assignments here and there doing a story for *NBA Today* or a live shot for the NFL Network. College football sideline reporting is an interesting position because although I enjoyed being at "the big game," I spent an inordinate number of hours and days researching and preparing stories for 25-second reports. It started to feel like my work wasn't adding value to the show, and I noticed a drop in my feeling of fulfillment. Some might wonder if work is supposed to be fulfilling every minute of every day. Isn't that unrealistic?

**CONFIDENCE SPROUTS WHEN YOU DO DIFFICULT THINGS. IT GROWS WHEN YOU REPEATEDLY TAKE ON CHALLENGES.**

Yes and no. There will certainly be days when an aspect of your new life is frustrating or unsatisfying. I like to reevaluate when the scale tips to more unsatisfying days than fulfilling days. This has been a huge key to helping my career evolve. When I feel discontent creeping in or a lack of motivation, I don't push it down but welcome and examine it. Usually a motivated person who takes pride in researching and doing a great job, I knew it was time for a change when I felt like cutting sideline game preparation short because "none of it would make air anyway."

It's in moments like this when the audacious identity takes over. I had already faced my fear barrier once when I moved from behind the scenes to in front of the camera. I had already made friends with fear, and it was time for me to call that old friend again. Change is always scary, but with the reevaluation loop, you can have confidence when making decisions to change course, simply because you've done it before. It will never be your first time again. Confidence sprouts when you do difficult things. It grows when you repeatedly take on challenges. Your audacious mindset, behavior, and identity converge to allow you to take an unflinching look at what is and isn't working.

After college football sideline reporting for two years, I began to suspect the position had a potentially short shelf life. I couldn't see a path to elevate my career from that position. Moving from sideline to studio anchor or play-by-play commentator isn't common. Everyone, it seemed, wanted to be a sideline reporter! Fresh college graduates would enter the profession, work for a lower fee, and do just as good a job (or sometimes better) than I. Most sideline reporters stay in the position until they are replaced. There are, of course, exceptions to any rule, and some have made entire careers out of excellent work on the sidelines. But I didn't see that as my future—I couldn't envision it. Sideline reporting felt like a step in my professional journey rather than a destination.

In 2005, new cable networks were popping up both regionally and nationally. Alongside that, programming grew a need for more live event announcers. When you watch a game on television, a play-by-play commentator usually delivers the mechanics of what is happening and keeps track of time and situations, accompanied by an analyst or expert in the sport, who is responsible for communicating the why and how of a particular action. CBS had a new network called College Sports Television (CSTV) with the programming consisting entirely of college sports. I had been a Division 1 collegiate volleyball player, so I approached them, inquiring about being an analyst on their college volleyball matches.

My first assignment was at the mecca of college volleyball, the University of Nebraska, where I was assigned to work with Jason Knapp, a versatile and talented multisport play-by-play announcer. By the first commercial break, I knew this was the lane for me. It still required many days of research and preparation, but instead of trying to condense my ideas into 20-second hits, I was able to explain and share them over the course of a two-hour game.

After returning from that first weekend in Nebraska, I told my friends, "It is what we already do—watch a match and talk about it!" That was a simplistic way of looking at it, but it was energizing, and it solved my problem.

The problem was twofold. First, I knew I could be easily replaced on the sideline. As a collegiate volleyball analyst, you had to at least have played and understood the college game. I was qualified, and that separated me from the masses. My second problem with sideline reporting was constantly feeling like 99 percent of my research was left unshared as I tried to fit it into 25-second hits. As a live event announcer, my partner and I had hours (not seconds) to educate and entertain the audience.

## Not Every Move Is a Life-Quake

There is a difference between upending your life to move cross-country without the promise of employment (as I did when moving to the beaches of Southern California) versus making some professional tweaks to reignite your desire to do good work. Shifting to work as an analyst was a professional tweak: I still kept sideline reporting but added calling live events as a volleyball analyst in my television rotation. Each week, I would do two to three games, some football sidelines and others as a volleyball analyst.

I'm always trying to stay slightly ahead. It is what drives my FOSS (fear of staying the same). A few years after calling volleyball games as an analyst, I saw that other former volleyball players were positioning themselves to be television analysts too. Holly McPeak, an NCAA Champion, three-time Olympian, and bronze medalist, lived just down the street from me. I knew if I wanted to keep working in volleyball, I needed to move over to play-by-play— an Olympic medalist would understandably get hired over me if we were competing to be an expert in the same sport. At that time, there were very few women working as play-by-play announcers. It was time for another audacious move, and with that, I pushed to change roles and added sports to my roster of events. As a play-by-play announcer, I wasn't limited to volleyball but could work with experts from many different sports. I dove into studying basketball, softball, soccer, water polo, track, and field. I enjoyed working with analysts

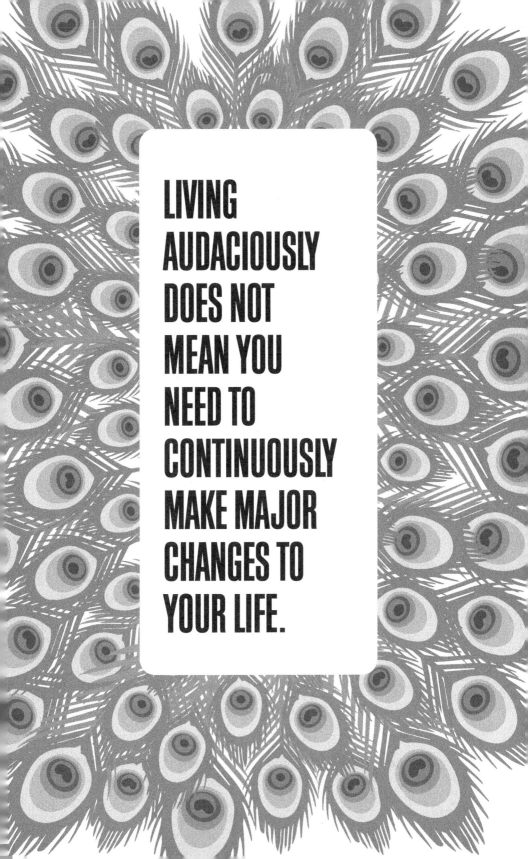

LIVING AUDACIOUSLY DOES NOT MEAN YOU NEED TO CONTINUOUSLY MAKE MAJOR CHANGES TO YOUR LIFE.

in each of the different sports I called and felt reenergized yet again by the growth it required.

Living audaciously does not mean you need to continuously make major changes to your life. You just need to be tuned into what is and isn't working. Sometimes, it is as small as changing your work hours; other times, it is a complete overhaul of a specific area of your life you find unsatisfying.

Enter the reevaluation loop, which is exactly what it sounds like—taking the time to reevaluate your situation to ensure it is still serving you. When should you begin reevaluating? Everyone has a different threshold. I give discontent a fairly short leash before beginning the reevaluation process. After feeling a grain of irritation, I start. Maybe a minor tweak can fix whatever is nagging me. If not, it is time for me to dive deeper. Others who might be new to an audacious way of living or have a lower tolerance for risk will likely have a different flash point. There is no right answer.

Try using the Contemplation Cs below to gauge if an adjustment is needed.

## The Contemplation Cs

### Clarity

Do you have a clear picture of what you want to accomplish? In chapter 2, we vetted your idea and clarified what you want in your audacious life. Are you receiving those things you wanted? More time with family, freedom, money, joy, or whatever you envisioned? There is nothing wrong with adjusting the plan if what you want has changed or evolved. We all grow at different rates. Perhaps you should revisit the ikigai principle or fill out a new Freedom Funnel. Examine what currently lights your fire. It is essential to have clarity on what you want from your life, and if you aren't getting it, to explore what it is you do want. And it is ok if it changes—you don't have to stay the same!

## Capability

Are you capable of following through on your goal in your current situation? This question does not mean you should invite your inner critic over for dinner and let it talk you out of audacity! But if, for example, you want to be an African wildlife photographer and you're also a single parent to young kids, that will affect your capability for now. Not forever, just for now. If you aren't capable of following your original path, don't stop—just reevaluate and find the things you can pursue toward that goal. Photography in a different form, perhaps, until you can go overseas. Portraits, pets, or creating a collection of African wildlife photographers' best work are some of the varied options that might work until you have more flexibility in your schedule.

Audacity isn't about throwing caution to the wind and neglecting your other duties. Audacity is about constant reevaluation in the pursuit of your goals, and as what you are capable of changes, you need to be flexible.

## *Capacity*

What tools are you missing that might make pursuing your dream more reasonable? Capacity is about asking yourself, "Do I have everything I need to get it done?" Do you need more training than you currently have? If so, seek it out. Have you connected with people adjacent to what you want to do to explore collaboration? Perhaps you need more capital to do your work. If so, revisit your financial budget for areas you can cut back, study creative ways to get sponsors, or search for more economical means to accomplish your goals.

## *Consistency*

Are you consistent in your efforts? If you want a large Instagram following for your business, you must post the right content regularly. If you want to attain your real estate license, you need to study for the test a little bit every day. Your balance between what is urgent and important is critical. Even if you have a very full life, consistently putting in a little bit of time, money, and energy will move you closer to your goal. One step a day will eventually add up to an entire marathon. Even if the day prior feels like you didn't make any progress or had a backward slide, it is critical to be consistent. Some days will have significant gains, and others will feel hopeless. Keep going.

## *Celebration*

Celebrate victories along the way. Decades ago, when I climbed to Everest Base Camp, I did not save my sense of accomplishment for the arrival. I acknowledged progress every evening, no matter the distance covered. If you are only going to celebrate when you reach your proverbial peak, it might be tempting to give up along the way because the goal will seem so far away.

Sometimes, in this celebration phase, your discontent may be resolved. Perhaps you have made amazing progress toward your new life but have not taken the time to notice how far you've come. Once you recognize and honor the work you have already done, you may find renewed energy. I gave myself a pat on the back every time I turned in two chapters of this book for review. If I had only celebrated when the book was published, I suspect the year writing it would have been overwhelming.

### Critical Conversations

After examining the first four Contemplation Cs, it is time to have some critical conversations with yourself and maybe one or two of those most trusted in your front row. Do you need to head in a different direction? I do not mean stopping, returning to life as it was, and staying stuck. Never! But if you aren't enjoying your life, take steps to improve it.

Ask your inner circle what they see. Are you happier? What have they observed about your capability, capacity, and consistency? You avoided filling your front row with yes-men for this reason. Invite constructive criticism and be willing to take it. It doesn't mean you have to do the first thing your chosen squad member suggests, but as you ask for feedback from people you trust, pay attention to reoccurring themes.

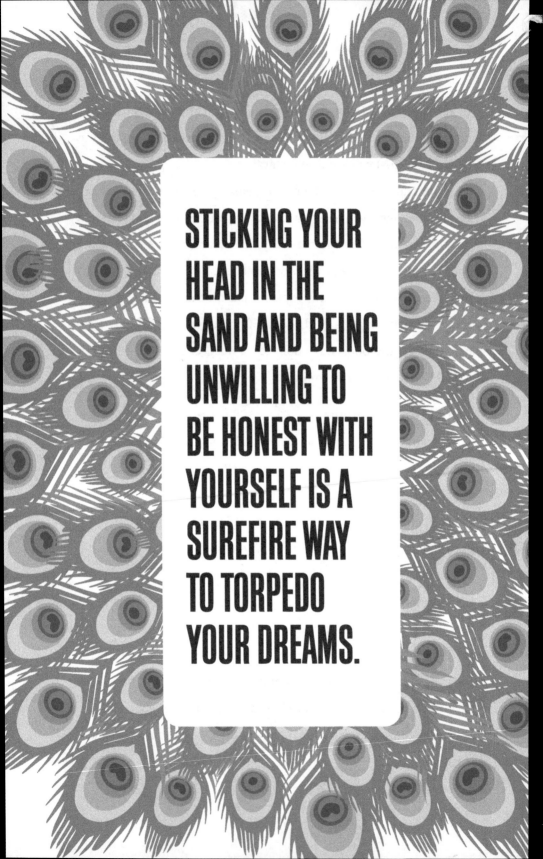

STICKING YOUR HEAD IN THE SAND AND BEING UNWILLING TO BE HONEST WITH YOURSELF IS A SUREFIRE WAY TO TORPEDO YOUR DREAMS.

Sticking your head in the sand and being unwilling to be honest with yourself is a surefire way to torpedo your dreams. Don't do it.

## Audacious Assessment: Navigating Toward Fulfillment and Growth

As you work through the reevaluation loop and ponder on the Contemplation Cs, you can also use the assessment below to help gauge where you are in your journey and if that direction is working for you.

**Instructions:** For each question, select the answer that best reflects your current situation. Assign points to each response based on the scale provided. Total your points for each category at the end to determine your recommended course of action.

## CAREER AND PROFESSIONAL DEVELOPMENT

**1. How much joy do you find in your current role?**

☐ I'm very happy and look forward to work every day (5 points)

☐ Moderately happy; most days, I'm excited to go to work (3 points)

☐ Somewhat happy but other days I don't enjoy it (1 point)

☐ I don't look forward to it at all (0 points)

**2. Do you feel challenged and stretched in your professional endeavors?**

☐ Absolutely, I'm constantly pushing my limits (5 points)

☐ Mostly, but there's room for more challenges (3 points)

☐ Not really, I'm comfortable in my routine (1 point)

☐ No, I feel stagnant and unchallenged (0 points)

### 3. Are you making progress toward your career goals?

☐ Yes, I'm actively working toward my goals and seeing results (5 points)

☐ Somewhat, but I could be more focused (3 points)

☐ Not really, I'm unsure of my direction (1 point)

☐ No, I feel stuck and directionless (0 points)

# RELATIONSHIPS AND PERSONAL CONNECTIONS

### 1. How satisfied are you with the quality of your relationships?

☐ Extremely satisfied, my relationships are enriching and fulfilling (5 points)

☐ Mostly satisfied, but there's room for improvement (3 points)

☐ Somewhat dissatisfied, I feel disconnected from some people (1 point)

☐ Very dissatisfied, my relationships are strained and unfulfilling (0 points)

### 2. Do you feel supported and valued by your loved ones?

☐ Absolutely, I have a strong support system (5 points)

☐ Mostly, but there are times when I feel overlooked (3 points)

☐ Not really, I often feel unsupported (1 point)

☐ No, I lack support from my inner circle (0 points)

### 3. Are your relationships conducive to personal growth and development?

☐ Yes, my relationships inspire me to grow and evolve (5 points)

☐ Somewhat, but there's room for deeper connections (3 points)

☐ Not really, my relationships are holding me back (1 point)

☐ No, my relationships hinder my personal growth (0 points)

# LIFESTYLE AND WELL-BEING

**1. How satisfied are you with your current lifestyle?**

☐ Very satisfied, I lead a balanced and fulfilling life (5 points)

☐ Moderately satisfied, but there are areas for improvement (3 points)

☐ Somewhat dissatisfied, my lifestyle could use some adjustments (1 point)

☐ Very dissatisfied, my lifestyle is unhealthy and unfulfilling (0 points)

**2. Do you have sufficient time for activities that bring you joy and fulfillment?**

☐ Yes, I prioritize my passions and hobbies (5 points)

☐ Sometimes, but I often feel stretched for time (3 points)

☐ Rarely, I struggle to find time for myself (1 point)

☐ No, I have no time for personal activities (0 points)

**3. Are you managing your finances in a way that aligns with your values and goals?**

☐ Yes, I have a clear financial plan and stick to it (5 points)

☐ Somewhat, but I could be more disciplined (3 points)

☐ Not really, I struggle to budget and save (1 point)

☐ No, my finances are a source of stress and uncertainty (0 points)

**Assessment Scoring**

Total your points for each category: career and professional development, relationships and personal connections, and lifestyle and well-being. Evaluate each category separately, taking note of any imbalances. Are you a high scorer in relationships and personal connections but far lower in lifestyle and well-being? Is your career and professional development highly satisfying but your relationships score reveals a lack of connection? It is possible that you are highly satisfied in one area while another is dragging you down. For an overall picture, add the points from all of the categories together. Use the following scale to determine your recommended course of action:

**35–40 points: No Change Needed.** Your life is on track and flourishing. Keep up the excellent work!

**25–34 points: Small Tweaks.** There are minor areas that could use improvement. Focus on making small adjustments to enhance satisfaction and growth.

**15–24 points: Significant Shifts.** There are notable areas of dissatisfaction that require attention. Consider making significant changes to improve satisfaction and progress.

**0–14 points: Complete Overhaul.** Your current situation is not fulfilling or conducive to growth. It's time for a complete overhaul to lead a more satisfying and fulfilling life.

The goal isn't to always be in the "No Change Needed" category. Ideally, if I have been diligent in reevaluating, I want to move between that and "Small Tweaks," with maybe one "Significant Shift" every 7–10 years.

Once you engage in a reevaluation loop, you may find the periodic examination of your life enjoyable. Some people go on a retreat every year or two, alone or with friends, during which they self-reflect. My evaluation is a continuous process; I am hyperaware of how I feel physically. My body provides lots of signs when I need a change, such as tending to lose focus doing work I used to love or feeling slightly depressed and wanting to take more naps. The discontent goes away when I try something new and returns when I go back to my normal routine.

Whether your process is separating from your daily routine or having a rolling conversation with yourself, being aware of how your life is working for you is crucial. Cultivating audacity is not about making one move. A truly audacious and satisfying life is always under construction. The future you is depending on the current you to keep the promises you made to yourself yesterday. Making the audacious move isn't the end of the story. It is the beginning.

# THE FUTURE YOU IS DEPENDING ON THE CURRENT YOU TO KEEP THE PROMISES YOU MADE TO YOURSELF YESTERDAY.

## — UNKNOWN

What I don't want is for you to read this book and say, "Yes, but . . ." Yes, but . . . what? The answer to that question is what stands between you and creating a life you are excited about, leading straight to your primary barrier. If you still feel your feet on that sticky floor, catastrophize your hesitation. Take it to the very worst scenario where you die destitute and alone. Then take it to the best possible outcome with some blue-sky thinking: You are named Person of the

**WE HAVE TODAY AND NO GUARANTEE OF TOMORROW.**

Year by *Time* magazine. You win the Pulitzer Prize. You create a business or brand that changes the way the world works. Then, ponder the more likely outcomes that fall between those poles.

There is a lot we don't know in life, and much we can't control. We don't know how long we have to live, who we will live it with, what our future entails. But we have today—and no guarantee of tomorrow.

This book began with my experience of helplessly trying to save Peter as he suddenly passed away on the ESPN newsroom floor at only 37 years old. When the death rattle signaled Peter's life was over, I became acutely aware that his body had only been a container for his soul: He was no longer in the body before me on the floor. And then, as Peggy and I performed CPR, trying to revive him, I heard Peter's voice over my shoulder, saying, "Oh, you are so sweet; you don't have to do that."

I don't exactly know what my beliefs were about what happens after death before that experience, but now I know souls exist. And when Peter's soul left his body with that final expiration, his body was no longer recognizable. It looked like a mannequin—it was the shape of a body but only a replica. I sat on my knees, watching the paramedics take him away and tried to make sense of the voice I heard. I thought, *How could this possibly be the end of Peter's story? He had just gotten married, landed his dream job, and was fit, healthy, and young. What dreams did he have that were unrealized?*

# WHAT DREAMS DO YOU HAVE THAT LAY DORMANT?

What dreams do you have that lay dormant? What will your life look like if you never try? What could it be if you do? An audacious mindset is believing everything will work out as it should and that you'll be ok no matter the outcome. Audacious behavior is taking action toward your dreams. And an audacious identity is living with the awareness that tomorrow isn't guaranteed.

You picked up this book for a reason. What was it? Cultivating audacity releases us from an end point: It is not too late to take steps toward realizing your dream, and your dream is not too big. You are ready, and you have everything you need. This *is* the right time. Turn the page to a new chapter in your life.

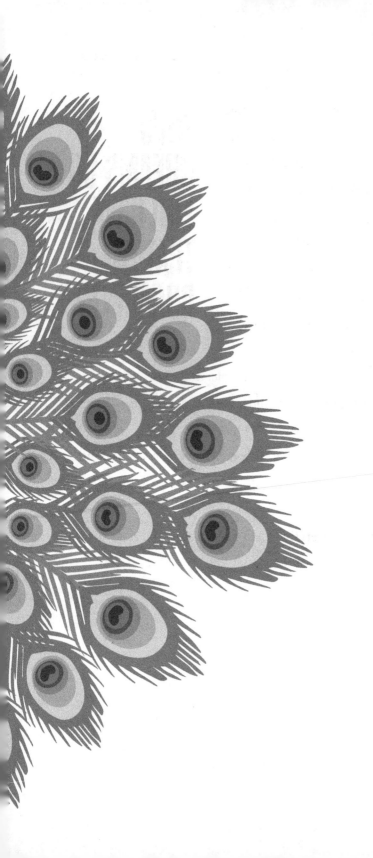

# DISCUSSION QUESTIONS

Discussion questions to explore with your front row, your book club, or your bestie. Making it public is an important part of the process!

## CHAPTER 1: THE POWER OF AUDACITY

- What do you feel in your body when you think about making a big change in your life?
- What comes to mind when you hear the word *audacity*?
- Where are you on the audacity continuum? Reflect on your behavior over the last five years. Have you made any decisions that surprised your friends? Were you someone who used to behave audaciously, but time has tamed you?
- Consider your identity. Simply put, who are you? How do you fit into your social circles? Ask those in your discussion group how they would describe you as it pertains to audacity.

## CHAPTER 2: YOUR TWO LIVES

- The first step to becoming audacious isn't just identifying what you want to do but why you want to do it. What is your motivation? (Better lifestyle? More money? Control of your schedule? More time with your family? Recognition from others?) How will you feel about yourself after you take the audacious leap?
- Consider what your life might look like after your audacious move. What will change? What will stay the same? What will you keep, and what will you let go?
- Create your own Freedom Funnel. Start by making four columns with one of the following questions at the top: What do you enjoy? What are you good at? What does the world need? What can you get paid for? (If in a group setting for this discussion, I suggest everyone have a piece of paper and make columns under those questions. Give one minute to write down everything that comes to mind without editing and use the entire minute! Then share.)
- Will the audacious move you want to make give you more of what you enjoy?
- If you let comfort or fear dictate your path and stay stuck, what might that look like? How would you feel if you never tried?

## CHAPTER 3: IDENTIFYING BARRIERS

- In seven words or less, state the story/limiting belief you've been telling yourself that is keeping you from doing the work to get you where you want to be.
- What constraints are keeping you in your current situation?
- After reading part 2 of this book, which barriers resonate with you? Fear, time, money, or your inner critic? It can be more than one.

## CHAPTER 4: MAKE FRIENDS WITH FEAR

- What scares you? Rejection? Failure? Embarrassment? Judgment? Or something else entirely?
- What is your greatest fear pertaining to this move? How can you actively seek it out to overcome the fear?
- Who are you currently giving a vote to, and from whom are you seeking validation?
- How can you ensure the changes you make are not based on seeking external approval?
- How do you define failure specific to your situation? Is it a failure if you learn from it?
- Reflect on past instances where fear held you back. What opportunities were missed due to fear?
- Consider the cost of allowing fear to dictate your choices. Does the pain of your current circumstances outweigh your fear of the unknown?

## CHAPTER 5: THE URGENCY FALLACY

- What are some examples of urgent tasks in your daily life that can wait 15 minutes while you prioritize what's important?
- How do you really spend your time? Keep a log each day for a week. Which times stress you out? Bring you joy? Energize you?
- Look at the visual representation of your time and reflect on your current commitments. Can some of it be adjusted or eliminated to hold space for the life you are creating?
- In assessing your time audit, consider if your pride is getting in the way. Can you hand over some of your load to someone else and better use that window of opportunity?

## CHAPTER 6: MONEY: TIME'S TWIN

- What's your money story? Think back to when you were growing up. What were the discussions about money like in your household?
- We all need to make a conscious decision: Are we going to remain stagnant in our relationship with money, or are we willing to invest in deconstructing that story and building a new one? What are your first steps toward deconstruction and rebuilding your story?
- What would your life look like if you allowed yourself to have an abundance of wealth?
- What money story are you passing on to your children?
- After tracking your spending, identify areas for adjustment. Are you sufficiently funding your audacious goals and the things that are important to you? In which categories are there opportunities for optimization and improvement?

## CHAPTER 7: THE INNER CRITIC

- What does your inner critic say most often? If you pick apart those thoughts without emotion, is there any grain of information that might be helpful?
- What name did you give your inner critic (and why)?
- What mantra, visual cue, or physical reset can help you manage your inner critic?
- If you could speak to your inner critic like Elizabeth Gilbert did to hers, what would you say?
- Share an example of something your inner critic has whispered to you. After reading this book and becoming aware of your thoughts, do you believe that message? How was the thought distorted? How has your perception of that comment changed?

## CHAPTER 8: HOW TO PACK YOUR PARACHUTE

- Reflect on what you learned about the barriers in chapters 4 through 7. What support do you need to feel more comfortable surrounding those obstacles?
- What fears did you identify? To pack your parachute, say those concerns aloud. Will you really die destitute and alone, or will the outcome, even in a poor situation, fall short of complete ruin?
- What time constraints did you identify? It is important that you clearly define what is important to you and allocate time accordingly. What plan are you packing into your parachute to ensure that happens?
- What did you discover as you examined your money story? Can you trade money to have more time or energy to pursue your goal? What steps do you need to take to reallocate that money toward your goals?
- As you get closer to taking the audacious leap, what have you observed about the frequency and types of messages your inner critic whispers (or screams) to you?
- Who are the people who want to see you succeed without jealousy?
- Who will talk you off the ledge of uncertainty and imposter syndrome, even when you don't want to hear it?
- Who will you invite to be in your front row for your audacious journey?

## CHAPTER 9: JUMP!

- You can't make your audacious move all in one day, but you can take at least one step. What will your first step be? How can you make that step public?
- What specific needs can you communicate to your front row?

- Whatever you need to do to take that initial leap needs to have a date attached. When and what will you do?
- Are you meeting your set goals? If not, does your goal or your plan need adjustment?

## CHAPTER 10: THE REEVALUATION LOOP

- Everyone has a different threshold for determining when they should enter the reevaluation loop. What feelings trigger your reevaluation process?
- Do you have a clear picture of what you want to accomplish? Will you receive the things you wanted? More time with family, freedom, money, joy, or whatever you claimed you wanted?
- Are you capable of following through on your goal in your current situation? If not, what do you need to be able to make progress?
- Who can you connect with adjacent to what you want to do to explore collaboration?
- Are you consistent in your efforts?
- Do you need to pivot in a different direction? Ask your inner circle what they see. Are you happier? What have they observed about your capability, capacity, and consistency?

# ENDNOTES

1 West, Missy. Interview. By Anne Marie Anderson. April 30, 2024.

2 Gassner Otting, Laura. *Limitless.* Ideapress Publishing, April 2, 2019.

3 Fisher, George. *The American Instructor, or Young Man's Best Companion: Containing, Spelling, Reading, Writing and Arithmetic, in an Easier Way Than Any Yet Published.* Forgotten Books, August 24, 2018.

4 White, Alexandria. "73% of Americans Rank Their Finances as the No. 1 Stress in Life, According to New Capital One CreditWise Survey." CNBC Select, May 20, 2024. https://www.cnbc.com/select/73-percent-of-americans-rank-finances-as-the-number-one-stress-in-life/.

5 McLeod, Saul. "Freud's Theory of Personality: Id, Ego, and Superego." Simply Psychology, January 25, 2024. https://www.simplypsychology.org/psyche.html.

6 Ibid.

7 Ibid.

8  Loder, Sandy. "The Impact of 45,000 Negative Thoughts." Peak Dynamics, March 10, 2023. https://insights.peak-dynamics.net/post/102ia4i/the-impact-of-45-000-negative-thoughts.

9  Gilbert, Elizabeth. *Big Magic: Creative Living Beyond Fear*. Riverhead Books, September 22, 2015.

10  *Collins Dictionary* (online). "Definition of 'Cocky.'" *Collins Dictionary* (online), 2024. https://www.collinsdictionary.com/dictionary/english/cocky#google_vignette.

# ABOUT THE AUTHOR

Anne Marie Anderson is a three-time Emmy Award–winning broadcaster, keynote speaker, and author. As she walked through ESPN's doors fresh out of college, Anderson embarked on a career that led her into the boardrooms and locker rooms of some of the nation's most successful sports franchises. Utilizing the methods observed from behind-closed-doors coverage of sport's high-performing coaches, athletes, and executives, Anderson applied their penchant for taking bold and sometimes surprising risks to her personal and professional life.

The knowledge and experience gained from making one surprising career move after another led Anderson to become one of the country's most experienced female play-by-play announcers. In *Cultivating Audacity*, Anderson shares the system she developed to find the courage to confront her hesitation and break down the barriers between her and the life she wanted.

Anderson is a highly sought-after keynote speaker and emcee. Delivering keynotes that are alternately funny and touching, she seeks to connect with the audience through the power of storytelling.

# WORK WITH ME

My hope is that this book is not something you read and then say "Yes, I will do that when I am ready." You are ready now. That is the entire point!

The concepts in these pages are not just applicable to individuals but also a road map to the development of elite organizations. I help corporate, educational, and athletic teams build rockstar cultures by weaving individuality into a powerful unit. I am all about customization. Before I speak to any group, we do an in-depth discovery call to learn your pain points and goals to then formulate a plan. I do not just repeat the same keynote over and over. My goal is to help YOU specifically get where you want to be.

As a private coach, I work with executives to identify the path to becoming a shape-shifting leader who connects with every squad member and fosters invested teamwork.

Simply put, these guidelines can transform disengaged employees into elite performers. If that sounds like something you would like to explore further, please contact my team at media@ annemarieanderson.com.

If you would like to order copies of *Cultivating Audacity* for your group, we can arrange a bulk discount.

Let's connect!

annemarieanderson.com

media@annemarieanderson.com

in @https://www.linkedin.com/in/anne-marie-anderson-3557ab39/

Instagram @Cultivating_Audacity

Facebook Cultivating Audacity

# ACKNOWLEDGMENTS

I had just finished delivering a keynote about audacity at a women's leadership event in Vermont in the fall of 2023 when a woman in the audience raised her hand and innocently asked, "What's next?" I responded, "I am going to write a book about audacity." There it was. I had said it aloud. A simple post-talk Q&A set this book in motion.

I am indebted to all those who have spent time sitting in my various front rows. You have cheered, pushed, challenged, supported, and lifted me up over the years. And you have inspired me with your own badassery.

First, my children: Lukas, Grant, and Leyna, I had no idea parenting was going to be this much fun. I learn grace, empathy, patience, forgiveness, and resilience from you and am so grateful you are my forever squad. Thank you for supporting me as I put important over urgently making dinner many nights over the past year.

Lukas, it has been such a gift to watch you grow into the man you are today. Confident, opinionated, and an absolute mental lock. The day you took me aside and coached me up as I was processing a rejection was the day the tide turned. Thank you—and yes, I am *a killer* and so are you. Can't wait to watch your next steps!

Grant, dude, you have taught me more than any human being on earth. You have this huge body and the softest heart of anyone I have ever met. You have an incredible ability to view the world from many different angles. It is a combination of a very sharp brain and an open mind. Your energy is unmatched and your capacity for empathy is humbling.

Leyna Mae, sister, we are just getting started. You are one of the brightest and most interesting people I have ever come across. Born with a smile on your face. I look forward to your nightly "fun facts of the day" and your endless hugs. Your future is limitless, and let me tell you, I am here for *all* of it. Front row sis, on anything and everything you need.

Thank you to my parents for introducing me to the concept of audacity when I was a know-it-all teenager. "You have the audacity to say that to me!" Dad—I finally did "the thing." The phrase you repeated throughout my childhood, "Do what you say you are going to do," has been a driving force in my path. So, when I finally said aloud that I was going to write a book, I knew it was happening. I felt your presence with me multiple times as I wrote these pages. That was cool. Come visit me in my dreams anytime. I love you.

Mama, 93 years old as of this writing, I am absolutely in awe of you. A tiny Italian immigrant who pushed me and supported me through every move. I must have made you crazy with my drama, complaining that I was too tall for school and too short for volleyball. There were so many times in my young life that you gave me the shove I needed. Thank you for being my cheerleader and watching endless sporting events on television just because I was announcing them. I felt guilty about working so much, knowing you stayed home with us, so when you told me you were proud of my career, it released me from fear of judgment. When things got tough, you always said "This too shall pass," and I learned that when things are great the same phrase applies. Just. Keep. Going. Don't worry, I won't tell my brothers that you said I am your favorite.

I was born lucky with four big brothers whom I adore. Ed, Dan, Steve, and Gary have had a seat in my front row from birth. Thank you for always taking my call, cheering me on, listening to my tears, helping me with life's big moments, and being my guys. You married well, and your wives are a constant joy in my life. I forgive you for locking me in the hotel bathroom with the heat lamp on. Multiple times. Also, Mom never said I am her favorite, but it is obvious, isn't it?

Matt, my ex-husband, parenting partner, and career front row. Had you not said "Take the job and we will figure it out," none of this would have ever happened. You have consoled me through so many rejections and listened to me endlessly catastrophize my fears. Indeed, we always figured it out. A true New Yorker who has had my back every step of the way. I am so proud of the partnership we have created.

To Val, without whom my career would not have been possible. I love you more than words, and you know why.

To Fabi, who agreed to be the director of operations of AMA Speaks LLC but probably didn't know that my ambitions were going to keep growing. Our Tuesday calls ground me, and I so appreciate your professionalism, forward-thinking, and friendship.

I have so many friends who have accepted, listened, pushed, consoled, supported, laughed, and cried with me without judgment over many decades. Holly, Ann, Megan, Helen, Jennifer, Joy, Mary, Nicole, Rushia, the volleyball girls . . . and many more. You are the best hype squad! Thank you for talking me off a ledge, laughing with me, letting me play and drop in and out of your lives. You are home base.

Thank you to my incredible work colleagues across multiple networks over the past 35 years, from whom I have gained strength, knowledge, grit, and friendship . . . the best part of my career has been working with you. It is an incredible gift to work with friends.

To the folks at The Speaker Lab, especially Erick Rheam, Maryalice Goldsmith, and Dan Alia. You and the entire team at TSL truly care about your students' success. For anyone reading this who wants to become a paid speaker, I can't recommend TSL any more highly.

To the incredible team at Ideapress—Rohit, Chhavi, Kameron, Megan, Allison, Marnie, Lynnette, Athena, Jessica, and the entire team. You made me feel comfortable from day one when I was a little bit skittish. Your creativity, kindness, and generosity were mindblowing, and I always left our calls so inspired. A little extra love for Kameron, who walked me through writing this book. I thought this was supposed to be hard, but you made it so enjoyable. Thank you.

For those of you who read the book (and the acknowledgments), sat in the audience, attended a workshop, and were eager to learn about audacity, thank you. I believe in every word of this book and know that if you spend your time taking bold, worth it risks pointing you toward a life (not just a job but a LIFE) you love, it will all unfold beautifully. Jump! You've got this.

Finally, a big thank you to all the noes, rejections, perceived failures, and fears in my life. Y'all inspire me to do more and be more every day. Bring it on.